Games Therapists Play

Games Therapists Play
How Punitive Diagnoses Allow the Fracture of Patient, Civil, and Human Rights -- with Impunity

Janet C. Saugstad

Universal Publishers
Boca Raton, Florida
USA • 2005

Games Therapists Play: How Punitive Diagnoses Allow the Fracture of Patient, Civil, and Human Rights -- with Impunity

Universal Publishers
Boca Raton, Florida • USA
2005

ISBN: 1-58112-455-4

www.universal-publishers.com

Contents

Dedication

My rapist got six months in prison and no psychiatric diagnosis.

I committed **no** crime and now have twelve psychiatric diagnoses.

My medical records state that I have three forms of depression, two neuroses, three personality disorders, three psychoses, and Personality 8, a diagnosis not even featured in the DSMIVR. I am the **only** person in the United States with Personality 8. **None** of the colleagues of the doctor who gave this diagnosis can explain it to me.

Why do I have so many diagnoses? I have complained to licensing boards eighteen times about unethical therapists. Fifteen times the various boards agreed with my complaint and slapped the therapists' wrists.

And the therapist has access to files **after** the board acts, so they retaliate with diagnoses lacking any basis in reality.

Chapter One – The Terror of Rape

Sexual assault occurs once every two minutes, according to the latest rape statistics. The Rape and Sexual Assault Center in Minneapolis, Minnesota provided this information. Seventy-two of each 100,000 women are raped each year. In 68% of these cases, the victim knew the assailant. Acquaintance rape is the most frequent at 35% percent. The next category of frequency is the boy friend at twenty eight percent. Family members are convicted in 5% of cases. That leaves 22% for stranger rapes, the Jack the Ripper stereotype.[1]

Rape experts across America remind the media not to think of the assailant as anyone out of the ordinary. Where it may be true that rapists may seem just like anyone else, that can't be said for certain. This is because the rapist is seldom required to seek psychological counseling.

After arrest, the court might require a psychological evaluation to determine the accused's fitness to stand trial. And after the victim has gone through the ordeal of trial, and the assailant is sentenced, the judge can order time in prison, or in-patient treatment, or incarceration in a state hospital, like the one in St. Peter, Minnesota.

Whether the assailant goes to prison, in-patient treatment, or incarceration in a state hospital, he can avoid mental health stigma, as he won't get a mental health diagnosis while serving time. The victim is the one that gets the "crazy" labels.

Is the treatment for sexual assault effective? Is the sex offender any less likely to re-offend once their in-patient treatment is complete?

Hardly. Alfonso Rodriquez, Dru Sjodin's murderer, spent most of his 23 years in prison in an in-patient program, but he received no new diagnosis while in this program. The only diagnosis he ever acquired was given him just a few months prior to his first offense in 1974. He saw a psychiatrist for depression and anxiety.

And treatment is not mandated in prison. In the case of Katie Poirier, the Moose Lake, Minnesota teenager, also murdered by a repeat sex offender, Donald Blum received no therapy and no psychiatric diagnosis.

The victim, meanwhile, is advised that s/he must stay in treatment for the rest of his/her life, especially if psychiatric medications have been prescribed. The victim is always the one who acquires the psychiatric diagnoses—and the resulting stigma. S/he is advised that s/he must do everything possible to ensure that the terror and anger resulting from this horrendous crime does not affect any of his/her relationships.

The violent act committed upon him/her is not prima-facie evidence of a twisted mind, however. The victim must take anger management courses and accept the labels given by medical personnel, who incidentally do not record anything in the medical record (after the initial psychosocial history) to explain any of the victim's continuing agony. All that appears in medical records is a list of symptoms that confirm whatever diagnosis has been submitted to the insurance company. These symptoms do not have to conform to the facts of the patient's life, either.

In the Katie Poirier and Dru Sjodin cases, their murderers had at least four previous convictions for rape. Yet neither of them had ever been extensively treated for **their** psychological problems.

And, whereas the court cannot order assailants to mental health counseling, if the victim should become hysterical in public for any reason, he or she can be court ordered. In some cases, the presiding judge in these court commitment cases will not even listen to opposing information provided by friend, family member or pastor.

In the case of Alfonso Rodriguez, his first conviction was in 1974, for sexual assault at knifepoint.[2] He was sent to St. Peter for six years. In Minnesota, some sex offenders are hospitalized rather than imprisoned. The reasons for this are explained as follows:

> The State of Minnesota uses two subdivisions of the Minnesota Commitment Act 3.to civilly commit sex offenders for treatment – the Sexual Psychopathic Personality provision and the Sexually Dangerous Person provision. A court

may commit a person for sex offender treatment if it determines that the individual is a "Sexual Psychopathic Personality," a "Sexually Dangerous Person," or both.

A Sexual Psychopathic Personality is a person who, as a result of a mental or emotional condition: (1) has engaged in a "habitual course of misconduct in sexual matters;" (2) has an "utter lack of power to control the person's sexual impulses;" (3) and, as a result of this inability to control his or her behavior is "dangerous to other persons."

A person can also be committed as a Sexually Dangerous Person. Unlike the Sexual Psychopathic Personality provision, a judge does not have to find that the person has an "inability to control the person's sexual impulses." A Sexually Dangerous Person means a person who: (1) has "engaged in a course of harmful sexual conduct" that creates a "substantial likelihood of serious physical or emotional harm to another;" (2) the person has a sexual, personality or mental disorder; and (3) the person is likely to engage in harmful sexual conduct in the future.[3]

Was Rodriguez' hospitalization anymore effective than imprisonment would have been? Within a few days of release, Rodriguez stabbed another woman and tried to kidnap her. Again, his only psychiatric diagnosis was for depression and anxiety. Depression and anxiety for rape and assault?

And the only treatment Rodriguez ever agreed to was for chemical dependency. It's useful for the felon, when appearing before the parole board, to show some willingness to change some aspect of his life.

After almost twenty-three years in state hospitals and prisons, Rodriguez was paroled on May 1, 2004. Six months later he was charged with Dru Sjodin's murder.

Here's the fascinating thing about his diagnoses for depression and anxiety. Mr. Rodriguez, and thousands like him, can obtain group therapy while on parole. Any rape victim also enrolled in treatment programs for depression never knows that a convicted rapist is making ceramics in her occupational therapy class at her Day Treatment program.

Therapists, who manage Day Treatment programs, make no effort to separate perpetrators from victims. Current laws in Minnesota, and most other states, do not require any public health program to be notified about anyone who might be a sex offender. The only thing that matters for Day Treatment programs is the diagnosis. Mr. Rodriguez would have had his ideal victim in such a program.

The only way a rape victim will ever know if her ceramics partner is a rapist, is if she decides to have coffee with him on her way home from the Day Treatment Program. People in his neighborhood have to be warned by law, but other patients in any Day Treatment or similar program are never informed.

Why is it important to say this? President Bush issued an Executive Order stating that all Americans be screened for depression. A teenager with poor grades might end up in such a program.

The public outcry over Dru Sjodin and Katie Poirier murders prompted the State of Minnesota to review its sex offender policies. The governor, Tim Pawlenty, made some spectacular promises in public about locking up sex offenders and thereby ensuring public safety, but then referred the matter to a blue ribbon commission. Usually when politicians don't want to deal with a problem, a commission is formed to study it to death.

This commission has come to some fascinating conclusions, however. It states, "For all of their talents and skills, social workers and psychologists do not have the specialized training to be effective supervision agents. When patients who have been civilly committed successfully complete treatment and are in transition back to they community, they need to be vigorously supervised by well-trained agents."

No such agent can be seen in any Day Treatment program where rape victims might encounter sex offenders. The mental health system makes most of its money by treating victims. It is therefore vital that people continue to view themselves as victims, and most therapists permanently place them in that role. I will support that statement in three ways:

1. I will show how therapists regard their clients from their own journal articles and books
2. I will tell my own story
3. I will retell the stories of other victims of abuse by therapists, by quoting published articles and books.

Chapter Two – Help to Heal?

I was living in Laurel, Maryland, when my neighbor broke into my mobile home one chilly November night and changed my life forever. During my long association with the U.S. military, I had been stationed in Maryland more than any other place. My ex-husband was a medical entomologist and Army officer. We had lived on military bases for most of the eighteen years that we were married, so there wasn't much equity in the house we had bought in Anne Arundel County.

Having been a full time mother for most of our married life, I was not making enough to do much more than squeak by. I had managed to earn a bachelor's degree between two duty assignments. But I had only begun to work in that field. My salary reflected my lack of experience. But I was making a name for myself – literally. And one of the perks of being an associate editor was having free passes to concerts and movies. It stretched my salary.

I didn't know my neighbor very well. I was a busy single mother, working for a newspaper in Annapolis, and participating in Toastmasters. That was better than any of the singles groups that seemed to be everywhere. They offered little in the way of friendships with the opposite sex – just a pairing off process that left a lot to be desired.

We were sharing custody at that time. The rape occurred when my son was with his father. Any other weekend that he'd be spending with his father would have been full of some kind of social activity, but that weekend my arthritis was flaring up.

I'd been in an automobile accident three years before that and had damaged my right kneecap, so I was on pain meds when Mr. Jackson entered my house unannounced. Whenever I had to take that drug, I could never sleep well. So I knew, at an intuitive level, the moment my neighbor entered my bedroom.

I woke up screaming as soon as he entered the bedroom. That surprised him, and he stood at the foot of the bed for an instant, as though in the sights of a gun. Too bad I didn't have one that night.

As he moved toward me, I braced against the hard headboard, trying to disappear into it, I guess. I should have continued to scream, but I was in shock. I tried to reason with him.

I knew instantly who it was, although I didn't know my neighbor well enough to remember his name. The mailboxes were outside, affixed to a long, flat bar. I'd seen him at the mailbox the day before. He'd noticed my limp as I approached, and I told him about the accident, and the fact that it only bothered me when the seasons changed.

As he came closer to the bed I could see that he was wearing black jeans and a dark blue windbreaker, like mechanics wear. It had his name emblazoned above his right pocket. I didn't know him well enough to even be sure where he worked or what he did for a living. I was so busy with my life, I didn't know much about any of the neighbors.

On the night of the rape, I tried to reason with him, reminding him of the pain I was in, to no avail. Even while I was pleading with him, I was also wondering whether he might have a gun or knife, and praying that he didn't.

My heart pounded as he climbed on top of me. He pressed his rough hand on my mouth and the fingernails dug into the corners of my lips. I couldn't breathe, and my heart pounded in my ears. I wondered if I would live through this horror. He smelled of machine oil and stale whiskey. And I almost threw up as he pressed into me.

"Shut up if you want to live," he growled.

Without removing his hand from my mouth, he slapped me so hard with the other hand that I fainted for a moment.

He did not need to tear my clothes as I was wearing a ragged old nightgown. I wasn't expecting anyone, and it was easy to use when I needed to put ice on my knee as a pain reduction device. He just pulled it up and unzipped – very neat and clean for him.

When I came to awareness again, he was grinding himself into me. My stomach churned and I shrieked. Again he slapped me and I went under.

The next time I woke, I pretended to still be asleep. His mouth was on mine as he drove into me. My stomach churned and I prayed he would be done soon and just leave. It was the worst feeling I've ever had.

It seemed like forever, but finally he stood, zipped up, and said, "Say one word and I'll be back."

"I won't," I promised, just wanting to be sure he'd go.

As soon as he left, I ran into the shower and let the warm water flood over me. I washed every part of me, until the water began to turn cold.

So began a frightening experience that would forever change my life. Over the next few weeks, the anger that he deposited inside of me would grow like a parasite. I began to devolve into a person I did not know. It took a major effort not to inflict my pain on my son.

At the hospital, the nurse who conducted the initial interview and took the samples for the court insisted that I contact the county rape crisis center for help in dealing with the fracture of rape. The groups were useful. Others in the same situation provided such compassion it was amazing.

But that rape center did not provide any advocacy for the interrogations by police. I went through all those endless personal questions by the police by myself.

I think the detective got a sexual thrill by asking some of the questions he asked. And the female officer assigned to the case after I protested was no better. At one point, she told me, "If you need someone to hold your hand through this, maybe you shouldn't go to court."

I could not believe how cold and hard she was. The male cop, I could understand. Corporal Hewitt was a real hard driving, macho guy. He obviously thought he was god's gift, the way he sashayed around. He even flirted with Agnes Moultrie, the cold, hard female officer.

It became clear that Cpl. Hewitt really didn't want to take this case to the county attorney. He made a practice of calling at work, and my boss asked if I had committed a crime. So I had to tell him that I'd been assaulted. I didn't say whether it was physical or sexual assault, but his attitude toward me had definitely changed.

In a way that was worse than the act itself.

I asked Hewitt not to call at work, as I'd like to be able to feed myself and my son for as long as possible, but that had no effect on him. A day after I made that request he called to set up another meeting.

He said he had talked to my neighbor, and had some follow up questions. When I asked if he had arrested the man and he said he couldn't do so until I answered these additional questions I said, "Oh that's wonderful. Just wonderful. He said he'd come back for me if I said anything. I could be long dead, by the time you decide to arrest him."

I think my boss heard that conversation, though he was in another room when that happened. I had to go stand outside for a while. I didn't want anyone at work to see my tears.

And I began to hate Cpl. Hewitt.

At our next meeting, I told him I knew he was walking all over my rights and that if he scheduled another meeting before arresting my neighbor I would bring an attorney with me.

Agnes Moultrie popped up with; "You don't need an attorney. Once it gets to court, the county attorney will represent you."

I cried. I couldn't help myself. "For it to come to court, I have to be alive. My neighbor could easily make sure I'm not. But I can't really afford an attorney, so I'll bring a tape recorder if I have to go through all these details again."

Cpl. Hewitt didn't hear me at all. Before the meeting ended, he checked his schedule and gave me another time. When I came in for another interrogation, he said, "The desk sergeant saw you with a tape recorder. Tape recording an officer of the law is against the law."

Fortunately my tape recorder was jammed, so I dumped out my purse on his desk, and said, "See, I don't have my tape recorder with me. I'd like the name and badge number of your desk officer. And I'm now in a place where I can file suit against you."

He back-pedaled so that his behind was almost out his office window.

I then said, "Look, if my neighbor is not arrested in the next twenty four hours, I'll splash this all over the front page of The Publick Enterprise and start an investigation of this police

station." (I was bluffing, as TPE was a business-oriented newspaper – part of the alternate press in Annapolis.)
Then I turned on my heel and left.
As I pulled into my driveway, a police cruiser pulled up next door. Moments later, my neighbor was finally taken into custody.
My neighbor sneered at me as he was loaded into the squad car. His wife gave me the finger. But I did not care. With him in custody, my sense of safety and my ability to sleep nights would grossly improve, and just the fact that I would not have to see Cpl. Hewitt again, was a blessing.
Was I imagining that the police did not want to arrest my neighbor? Not at all. It's still quite common for police to decide not to work all rape cases that are reported to them. The woman's movement has had little effect on this tactic. This is why the FBI can continue to state that violent crime is on the decline, when everyone knows otherwise.
The following table reflects data taken from a study available at www.rainn.org:

Reliability of FBI Rape Statistics

Police Dept.	Avoidance Tactics	Resulting Reports
Philadelphia	Use of code 2701	More than 700 cases not worked in five years
Phoenix	"Information only" cases	Up to 1/3 of cases not worked
St. Paul	"Cleared*" 108% of annual cases	Allowed city to claim 90% effective rate

- FBI reporting rules allow police to "clear" cases without arresting suspects
- Other cities solve about 1/3 of reported cases
Prior to this tragedy, I had had no psychotherapy. My ex-husband and I had about six months of marriage counseling, but were transferred to another base in the middle of it. But I took no

11

psychiatric diagnosis into the police interrogations or into the court case.

My character therefore, was not in question during the period between my neighbor's arrest and trial.

The stress of this trauma did not result in job loss either, at least not directly. A husband and wife team owned The Publick Enterprise. It operated on such a tight budget, that neither of them was covered by health insurance. When Margot required a mastectomy, two-thirds of the staff was laid off. The graphic artist was the first to be eliminated and I was the third.

Out of work, I took advantage of the time and went to stay with a friend in Northern Virginia. I did temporary office work while staying there. I needed time away from the neighborhood in which the crime had been committed. It was very rejuvenating, as she and her husband were renting a farmhouse and boarding horses to augment their other income. That meant I could ride after supper in exchange for grooming the horse and cleaning the stall.

Six weeks passed before the court contacted me for a brief meeting with the county attorney. That was easy to cope with, compared to the interrogations with the police. I repeated all the details just once and was given information on how the court functions. The docket was so full, it took almost eight months for the case to come to trial.

I was not required to maintain residence in the state in order for the case to go to trial. But even though I was keeping busy with clerical assignments, the situation was becoming difficult. I was a third wheel in Kathy's household.

So I found a job in the county west of Laurel, for another small newspaper. By this time, I was also referred to a psychologist for more intensive treatment than provided by the Rape Crisis Center.

Chapter Three - Another Kind of Rape

After completing the therapy program at the rape crisis center, I was referred to a psychologist as I was still having flashbacks. I was also told that while the trial was pending, it was vital that I continue treatment in order to avoid inflicting my agony on my family relationships and friendships.

The name on the business card I was handed was Joan Roberts Field, PhD. I was told that her use of hypnotherapy would help with my flashbacks without any need for medication. I like the idea that I would not need medication, so I made an appointment the next day.

Her office was in a large business complex that included lawyers, dentists, stockbrokers, and computer repair companies. It was lavishly decorated and had a view of the golf course. On the walls were prints of famous artists and her credentials framed in gold.

On a teak coffee table in her waiting room, was a copy of Baltimore magazine, featuring an article about Dr. Field. Her picture was on the front page of the magazine. The article chronicled all her achievements, including the most recent: first female president of the Maryland Psychological Association.

I therefore assumed that I had the best of the best.

If her peers held her in such high esteem that they elected her to run their professional organization, I was sure I had nothing to worry about. Of all the possibilities in that state, I had found the best qualified to treat my rape trauma.

As we began our sessions together, I had not passed through the probationary period at work and had no corporate health benefits. Fortunately, I did still have coverage from CHAMPUS (Civilian Health and Medical Program of the Uniformed Services) as my marriage to an army officer had exceeded ten years.

I had traded away my share of his retirement benefits, in exchange for a new car and five years of alimony. I was working at the time of our separation and could not predict the rape or any of its long-range consequences. I was hopeful that by the time the alimony expired I would have sufficient income to make it on my own.

But in order for Dr. Field to use my CHAMPUS benefits to pay for psychotherapy, she needed to submit a diagnosis. She chose clinical depression and posttraumatic stress disorder. PTSD is a common diagnosis for rape victims, and divorce leaves most people with some form of depression for some part of their lives. Being a single parent causes so much stress for both parties, and their children, that depression is quite common.

My marriage had lasted eighteen years. Now, more than half of marriages end in divorce and second marriages do not fare much better.

CHAMPUS allowed weekly sessions at that time, for the first six weeks, after which it would only pay for bi-monthly sessions. Dr. Field assured me that even though I had an incredible amount of stress as a single mother with a rape trial pending, there should be no problem complying with the framework established by CHAMPUS.

So we began counseling immediately. Hypnosis was very helpful in controlling most of the anxiety brought on by those arduous police interrogations. Self-hypnosis, at key times, resulted in a degree of relaxation that I still think allowed me to take care of my son without inflicting him with the deep anger I had toward both my rapist and the police.

I was very fortunate that I had a good support system. I lost no friendships during this period. Even though I was no longer an officer's wife, I still had a dozen friends I had made while traipsing all over the world.

Not only that, but I had remained friends with Margot and Frank, despite the lay-off from The Publick Enterprise. Margot had come through the initial stages of breast cancer and was adjusting well to the mastectomy and follow up chemotherapy.

And self-hypnosis was fun. It gave me a tool when the world started to crash in on me. I could ignore some of the stress as I dealt with the pain of rape. And the deep relaxation I got from trance also allowed me to continue to prioritize the things that needed to be done so that I didn't get overwhelmed.

But then one of Dr. Field's other clients committed suicide. She told me this over coffee at Clyde's, a restaurant favored by the movers and shakers in that part of the state. On my budget, coffee was the only thing on the menu that I could afford. But Dr. Field paid for our meal with her credit card.

I felt as though I was specially favored by having social contact with the president of the Maryland Psychological Association. I even hoped that she might introduce me to one of the lawyers that frequented Clyde's – someone with prestige and money.

As we waited for our meal, she described her anorexic client, Mary. I found out that Mary had grown up in an alcoholic home and had gotten no compassion or support from her parents. Her anorexia, according to Dr. Field, was a statement about her sterile environment. Controlling her food intake was a silent announcement of her extreme distress.

Then Dr. Field smiled and said that if Mary's parents had not removed her from treatment with her, that Mary would not have committed suicide. "She gained twenty five pounds while she was my client and her grades improved markedly in school."

She went on to say that she wanted to tell Mary's parents that at the funeral, but choked back the words.

I wanted to ask her if it was common for therapists to attend the funerals of their clients and add to the parents' misery, but I didn't want to be excluded from Clyde's and my chance to find a wealthy mate. Still, I was concerned about the fracture of Mary's confidentiality.

I ought to have called her on that; because in the weeks that followed, I began hearing about all of Dr. Field's other clients. There was Judy the Artist, who was so lacking in self-esteem that she would never get the promotions her talent should ensure.

This may or may not have been true. Dr. Field's undergraduate degree was in fine arts. Her first professional job had been as an apprentice to a visual artist, who only allowed her to mix colors for his murals. Since that was not very satisfying, and the salary was not suitable, she decided to become a psychologist.

There was Don the Snake-man, who had a penchant for sado-masochistic sexual activities. He was a successful businessman, and Dr. Field laughed about how adept he was at handling his secret life. Whenever I shared the waiting room with someone in a three-piece suit, I wondered if it was Don.

Spotting the Dresden Doll was very easy because she preferred pastel blouses and was withdrawn socially. Dr. Field also told me that her father was very critical of her when she was growing up. She could never do anything right in his eyes. He told her she would never amount to anything.

That was one of the reasons she decided to change from being an artist to being a psychologist. She decided that having a good salary would prove him wrong. Being able to drive a brand new Cadillac was one way in which she challenged her father's low opinion of her.

I began to wonder about **my** confidentiality and whether CHAMPUS should pay **me** to listen to all of her problems. I had essentially become her therapist. She told me about problems in her marriage, even interrupting a session to call her husband, to chew him out.

Then one day when I came for a session, I saw her pacing the floor and staring out the window. Someone she had helped convict had been paroled and had left a scary message on her answering machine.

It slowly became clear to me that despite her status as President of the Maryland Psychological Association, Dr. Field needed lots of help herself.

I asked a friend I'd known while I was an officer's wife, stationed in Japan. Cheryl had a master's in social work when she married Dale Simpson. She became a full time mother immediately thereafter and had never used her degree.

Cheryl and Dale were now stationed at Walter Reed Army Medical Center and had a nice house in Bethesda. I spent a Saturday with Cheryl and asked her what I needed to know.

She comforted me about the rape and said I should report Dr. Field to the licensing board, not only about breaches of confidentiality, but also for the dual relationship aspect of the code of ethics.

She explained that therapists are not supposed to have social contact while they are conducting psychotherapy. It has to do with transference, a necessary ingredient in therapy. Transference is the tendency to project unmet needs for affection unto the therapist. According to Cheryl, if handled correctly, it can assist the client in doing some real work. She then said I had a responsibility to myself and all of Dr. Field's clients to report her lack of ethics.

Cheryl said that I owed it to myself to find another therapist as my healing from that rape had been compromised by Dr. Field's problems. When I expressed some reluctance to do so, she said, "One bad apple does not spoil the barrel."

But Jeffrey Masson, in Against Therapy, says, "Abuse of one sort or another is built into the fabric of psychotherapy. The ways that a therapist can harm a patient are as varied as they are in any intimate relationship."[1]

My formal complaint to the licensing board resulted in another round of interrogations with three officials in the Department of Mental Hygiene.

And now, with another load of trauma, I was hospitalized for suicidal ideation. Though I had no symptoms of psychosis, I was given Mellaril in addition to Prozac, to control my nightmares.

I subsequently learned by reading Toxic Psychiatry, by Peter Breggin, MD, that psychiatrists commonly prescribe a low dose of an anti-psychotic in hopes that by so doing, Prozac's potential for making patients' violent, could be averted. So many murder cases have shown that Prozac and its sister medications can cause violent obsessions that this tactic has been shown ineffective.[2]

Basic Info provided by Toxic Psychiatry

Psychiatric med	Effectiveness	Side effects
SSRI antidepressant • Prozac, Zoloft, Luvox, Effexor, etc.	Equal to placebo	Increased suicidal ideation, gastric pain, weight gain, loss of libido
Neorolyptics – Anti-psychotics	Can increase hallucinations and delusions	Gross changes in gait, heart rhythm, kidney, brain damage
Lithium	Variable	Heart rhythm, kidney disease, birth defects

That was four years prior to the publication of Toxic Psychiatry, and I was not told this at the time I was medicated, despite all the informed consent provisions that are supposed to apply to all physicians.

Now I was told, despite this fracture by a therapist, that I would have to take an anti-depressant for the rest of my life. That also meant that I would need psychotherapy for the rest of my life.

At no time did any of the staff at that hospital discuss the ethics violation and all that stress. I was redirected to the rape, instead. The lack of ethics is **never** discussed, never treated like the deep fracture of trust that it truly is.

I know this on a personal level because I have filed against eighteen therapists and no therapist has ever discussed any part of the damage done by previous unethical therapists. Furthermore, in fifteen of those cases, the licensing board agreed with me, but the therapist was barely disciplined at all.

In the case of Joan Roberts Field, PhD, she lost no income from her practice. She was only required to take a twelve-credit course in ethics at the master's level. My complaint protected no other potential client, therefore.

Also, therapists are not required to study their own codes of ethics. Ethics courses at the master's level are merely a survey of ancient and modern philosophers. I took that course myself. I slept in class and got a decent grade.

And therapists are given access to client records after the board acts. That's why I now have twelve diagnoses. But therapists have gotten away with murder. Abuse of all kinds is common in the field. Read Against Therapy for all the details of how therapists can abuse their clients and get away with it.

The author, Jeffrey Masson, PhD and psychoanalyst, states that the founder of Gestalt Therapy, Fritz Perls, regularly beat his patients and was proud of it.[3] In his autobiography, he tells about how he fought with one of his female patients, knocking her down three times. "I've beaten up more than one bitch in my life."[4]

John Rosen, a psychoanalyst, had sixty-six counts of assault against him when the truth came to light. Most of them were for physical and sexual assault, but there were also three murders and four kidnappings.

Dr. Rosen surrendered his medical license and paid a $100,000 fine. He spent no time in prison and never lost his membership in the American Medical Association.[5] He got away with murder.

In his clinic, Delaware Valley Mental Health Unit, the use of cattle prods was quite common. Sex with patients was a regular staff benefit. Some of it was so grotesque; Dr. Rosen and his chief administrator ought to have been imprisoned just for those acts. One of Dr. Rosen's patients died of a ruptured liver, the result of having been beaten with a baseball bat.

But that book had not yet been published while I was in the hospital. And although that hospitalization lasted only a week, I ended up having to surrender custody. I had no family near me and no friend could be expected to provide childcare for days on end. If anything happened to my son, a power of attorney would be needed before he could be treated.

Losing custody was a deep, deep, pain, but I was assured that once on medication for a while, I could assert my parental rights again. With assistance from my psychiatrist, the court would probably view my case with approval. I wondered what it was that I did to deserve this. I had committed no crime or behaved unethically, but no one heard me.

My focus became getting out of the hospital. To do so as quickly as possible, I also agreed to quit my job and get on social security disability. That is one of the major tasks of medical personnel who derive most of their income from Medicare payments. But I didn't think about that at the time. I only knew the deep pain I was in.

I was referred to a husband and wife team for my follow up care. He was the psychiatrist, she the psychologist. I was assured that with "appropriate" treatment, I could regain my life.

At first, the medications did seem to make a difference. I slept like a baby. A bomb exploding outside my bedroom window could not have aroused me. But soon the suicidal thoughts returned and worsened. Anything that went wrong would elicit those thoughts.

I had lived with someone who was an entomologist and kept lots of insecticides in our garage. He also was a duck hunter and there were shotguns available, had I ever had any of those feelings before.

When I brought this up, I was told that it was simply the aftermath of rape, and not to worry. Prozac would eventually take care of it. Toxic Psychiatry and Talking Back to Prozac had not yet been written, but I started doing research on my medications anyway.

According to David Healy, MD, in Let Them Eat Prozac, "By the time Paxil and Zoloft came to market, further descriptions of SSRI akathisia, or suicidality were no longer scientific news."[6]

A study in the UK concluded that there seemed to be a suicide rate of between 44 and 64 per 100,000 patients. The rate of those on SSRIs seems to be 180 out of 100,000 patients, about three times that of placebos."[7]

But that study was reported in a medical journal not available in the public library. The only thing I could find dealt with the movement disorders: parkinsonosis and tardive dyskinesia.

When I asked my doctor about movement disorders, he became very angry. He said I was on such a low dose of Mellaril that I'd never have to worry about any changes to gait or movements.

Those changes could be quite grotesque, according to my readings. The tremors often resemble Parkinson's disease. But I was told not to worry, and just to trust my doctor to manage my medications.

Now poverty surrounded my life. Without a job and relying on social security, I thought about going back to Minnesota, for family support. But I wanted to see my son graduate from high school, so I stayed another year.

I ended up filing four more complaints, and wanted to leave therapy forever. I was told I could never survive without my medications and that therapy would help restore my life. I wanted to believe that. I truly did.

20

Chapter Four – Silence is Golden

I returned to Minneapolis and stayed with my mother for four months. When that arrangement became untenable, I got transitional housing through Lutheran Social Services (LSS.) My social worker at LSS insisted that I obtain more counseling at the Rape and Sexual Assault Center (RSAC). She did not even consider the deep fracture of my trust that occurred from the ethics problem with Dr. Field. She was solely concerned that the cross-country move probably worsened the trauma of rape.

Moving is stressful for some people, so it has to be for everyone. The fact that I had lived in a foreign country and moved seven other times in eighteen years was not taken into consideration.

As I've said before, it is difficult to maintain any sense of individuality in this inhumane system. Practitioners don't view their patient/clients as individuals, or their consciences might be invoked by all the abuse they visit on the people they supposedly serve. Since they view those they serve as objects, the person is encouraged to agree that they are not humans. It's a constant and subtle form of discrimination. (For evidence of this attitude, read chapter six.)

I did as I was told, however and made an appointment at RSAC. At that time, most of the counselors at RSAC were college interns, though clients were never informed of that fact. This means that the person conducting therapy has no real expertise in psychology or social work and may be using the client's story as part of the case studies for research papers for course requirements. And the degree does not even have to be in psychology or social work.

And sure enough, the counselor to whom I was assigned was a college intern. When I asked about her credentials, she lied to me. She stated that she was a staff member and supervised other therapists. She also stated that she was working on a master's in social work.

Her name was Karen Eckstrom. She was tall, slender, blonde and athletic. I actually believed she had the credentials she claimed to have, until the academic quarter drew to an end and she told me that she was leaving RSAC due to necessary back surgery. She said she expected a long recovery period.

About a week later, I came in to pay my small co-pay for my "treatment," and watched her descend two flights of stairs three stairs at a time. Then she zigzagged like an Olympic hurdler, through four lanes of traffic to reach a parking lot across a busy Minneapolis thoroughfare.

People who really need back surgery cannot move like she did, so the next day I called the director of RSAC and asked her about Karen's credentials. She apologized for the dishonesty of her staff member. But RSAC placed no disclaimer on any of their promotional materials, and made no new statements to incoming clients about their use of college interns.

So I contacted the Social Work Board. My complaint was investigated, and about three months later, I was told that Karen Eckstrom would not be licensed if she ever applied in Minnesota or Wisconsin.

Unfortunately, many of the jobs in social work do not require licensure. Someone with a Bachelor of Science in social work can assist clients in finding housing and make referrals to employment assistance programs. In fact, anyone with any kind of college degree can do this kind of work.

Therefore, denying a license to Ms. Eckstrom had little impact on her ability to harm other potential clients. This was not explained to me at the time, however.

I must say that the fact that she got away with her dishonesty at a Rape Crisis Center, until she lied to me, indicates once again how little respect most practitioners have for the rights of clients.

The composition of licensing boards also ensures that very few complaints will be investigated. Less than ten percent of the members of the board are representatives from the community, with no supposed ties to social work. However, having served on such a prestigious board cannot harm anyone's resume. And friendships are formed between the practitioner's and non-practitioners that have an affect on the quality of justice a complainant can receive.

About a year after my experience at RSAC, a group of clients filed a complaint having to do with a massive fracture of patient confidentiality. The focus of the complaint was that all college interns working at RSAC at that time had access to all patient records, and that case studies were being written by counselors who had had no contact with the clients being written about.

Shortly thereafter, a new line was added to intake forms, admitting that student interns were employed for most of the counseling sessions.

It is my assertion that the licensing boards do not exist to enforce the rules that are supposed to ensure that psychotherapy is a safe place to heal from life's tragedies. Furthermore, asking any profession to police itself is a prescription for disaster.

But I've also learned that politicians like Mary Ellen Otrembo, who is on a state committee that is supposed to provide oversight for mental health, will not investigate complaints made by clients of the mental health system. On paper, that is part of her job. But Minnesota derives about 1/3 of its tax base from employees of and programs within the mental health system. It is therefore important not to sully the image the state has worked so hard to cultivate: That is that Minnesota is the best place to send people with mental health issues.

But don't say this out loud is the message I've heard at the state legislature.

My experiences with the licensing boards in two states came **after rape,** a time recognized by most rational human beings as fraught with questions about whom to trust. A large part of the terror of rape is about the violation of the victim's safety, both inside their home and inside their bodies.

Yet the boards of social work and psychology in two states have admitted that my trust has been damaged over and over again by their practitioners. Again, nothing much has ever happened to these practitioners – **after rape.**

By far, the greatest damage done to my trust and my character were part of my ordeal at the Minneapolis Veteran's Administration Medical Center, to be discussed in detail in later chapters in this book.

In psychotherapy, the client is repeatedly admonished to be thoroughly honest. It's supposedly the only way to heal from whatever caused the "mental illness," in the first place. My experience tells me that the therapist is under no compunction to be honest at all.

And allowing therapists to comment on anyone's treatment records while the board is considering what action to take, ought to be unconstitutional. Where else in a free society can the party found guilty in a legal type proceeding attack the complainant? This makes those codes null and void, since punishing the patient for complaining means that there are no real consequences for therapeutic malfunctioning.

And the most insidious part of this outrageous practice is that the only way the patient will ever know that their records have been trashed is to take the time to read their own charts. Most patients don't do this. Therapists don't like patients who read their records. This supposedly indicates a lack of trust on the part of the patient. But it isn't really trust therapists want – it is blind faith.

I have also reported three physicians to the Medical Practice Board. The first was for the diagnosis of Personality 8 and his illegal subsequent action of barring my access to my own records.

The second complaint was for deliberate fracture of my patient confidentiality as I faced cancer of the vagina. The Medical Practice Board took no action, and I was told, "Doctor's are allowed discretion in applying the rules of conduct to patients in their care."

I will more fully discuss these two complaints in Chapter Seven and the third complaint for treating hypoglycemia as a full-blown psychosis, in Chapter Eight.

Chapter Five – In Harm's Way

Though my own service as an enlisted person was brief, compared to my eighteen years as an Officer's Wife, I was advised to contact the Veteran's Administration (VA) to file a claim for pensions and healthcare. My claim was rejected, and in order to file an appeal, I was told I would need a statement from my mother. She refused to give me that statement. That was no surprise to me as she has **never** been on my side.

Nevertheless, at that time, my category allowed an income of more than $25,000 before my eligibility for healthcare would be eliminated. I had already worked for a couple of temporary employment agencies and had hopes of returning to self-sufficiency. By obtaining healthcare at the Minneapolis VA hospital, I would have health care until corporate benefits would apply.

At that time, Social Security had no similar transitional program. In fact, after satisfying a nine-month trial period, my benefits would have been canceled. Now there is somewhat of a transitional period for social security in terms of healthcare and monetary benefits.

Since Toxic Psychiatry had not yet been written, I still believed that I would have to take my antidepressant for the rest of my life. So, even though I had already filed against ten therapists, and wanted to avoid them ad infinitum, I continued with my treatment for rape.

Doctor's of all types use subtle intimidation to help psychiatrists maintain the falsehood that depression must be treated with some kind of chemical antidepressant. But these doctors make a huge amount of money by treating all of the side effects. (The patient is never informed that they are side effects. Calling them stress-related illnesses blames the patient.)

Coincidentally, the VA had just launched a splashy public relations campaign announcing that female veterans could now obtain compassionate counseling for sexual assault. After having to file a complaint at RSAC in Minneapolis, I figured the VA could do no worse. I was in for the biggest surprise of my life.

The sexual assault specialist was located in the Veteran Services Center, on University Avenue in Minneapolis, about four miles from the hospital. This office was established primarily to assist homeless Vietnam veterans, though vets from other eras were not excluded. It also included a vocational rehabilitation program, for which I was not fully qualified, since I had yet to establish service connection. I was, however, able to use the computer to access jobs, and e-mail resumes, but not eligible for education or training.

I must admit that the social worker that was responsible for providing sexual assault counseling was **not** unethical. And unlike the "counselors" at RSAC, who were student interns, she had a master's degree and was licensed.

She had a good sense of humor, also. But she was obese. That made me wonder how effective her therapy was. She could give everyone else professional advice, but not take care of her own weight problem, using the techniques she was advocating. She was maybe 5'8" and at least 180 pounds.

It was when I went to a job interview, which I arranged from the Veteran's Service Center, that I had my first problem with Outpatient Psychiatry. In addition to the antidepressant I'd been taking for four years, I was also prescribed Buspar, to reduce the anxiety resulting from rape.

On the day of my job interview, I had a reaction to this drug. It was a hot day, and after a long bus ride to the job site, I almost fainted as I stepped off the bus. Nevertheless, after steadying myself, I managed to walk the two blocks necessary to reach the office where I had my appointment.

I stepped from 90-degree heat, into an air-conditioned office, which probably didn't help the situation. I moved slowly and carefully to the reception desk and checked in. I was handed an application and told to fill it out. So I found a chair and did so. When I stood up again to hand in the application, I got near the reception counter and fell to my knees.

The receptionist rushed from behind the counter and helped me to my feet. Once I was safely in a chair again, she called the on site nursing team. I was then asked a lot of embarrassing questions about alcohol and illegal drug use. I told them I'd gladly agree to any test to prove otherwise to be done immediately, if so desired. My blood pressure was taken and I was told that I was orthostatic. That can mean dizziness or dehydration, and can therefore be a serious complication. I was then told that I wouldn't be allowed to interview for the job until I had a doctor's notice allowing me to do so.

Sonja Williams, MD, did not want me to work at all. It was her advice that I continue to apply for Veteran's pension, ad infinitum, if necessary. When I tried to explain that my mother would not provide the statement required by the VA, she just smiled and said, "You should work with your county service officer."

I couldn't believe it. I had patiently explained all the reasons why my mother would not assist in my claim process, for at least five minutes. *And she gets paid for her listening skills,* I thought.

"Excuse me doctor, but that's where I got the information about the statement my mother has refused to provide."

There was therefore no chance that I could get a statement from any VA doctor that would convince any business to hire me. Besides, when I stopped in the public library on the way home, to read the information about Buspar in the Physician's Desk Reference (PDR), it said that one of the most frequent side effects of Buspar was dizziness.

The PDR is printed by the drug companies, and it is only the information agreed to with the Food and Drug Administration (FDA). In recent years, the FDA has removed several approved drugs from the market, some of which have been in common use for decades.

I was upset when I called Sue Peterson, RN, the nurse assigned to my case. The humiliation I suffered with a possible employer was not among her concerns. Nor was the side effect I had suffered. I said, "I think it's obvious that medical personnel have a much different definition for safe, than I do."

I asked for an immediate appointment with the doctor pertaining to this medication, but was told that it could wait until my next appointment, three weeks hence. Meanwhile, I was expected to continue to take the Buspar. I told her that was not possible.

She said, "All medications have side effects, and you have to learn to cope with them."

"Oh, really? What if it was your body and your physical health?"

I was told to calm down, as though I were a small child.

The next morning, I went to Outpatient Psychiatry and emptied my bottle of Buspar onto the floor near the reception desk. I said, "Tell you what, you take this so-called safe medication. I won't."

I then placed the empty bottle on the counter and left. By the time I got home, there was a message from Dr. Williams that I should call right away. When I did so, I was urged to return to the hospital and was admitted to Day Hospital. I was told that my blood pressure and blood sugars and medications would be evaluated.

The fact that I was receiving specialized treatment for sexual assault was part of my records. Not only that, but this was a pilot program, so anyone responding to the propaganda campaign, would be noted. Nevertheless, I was placed in a group where I was the **only** female participant.

Not only that, but every one of the male veterans had recent charges for physical assault: bar fights, domestic abuse and resisting arrest, to name just a few. I did participate for two weeks, until I was required to watch a presentation on the human reproductive system.

Now, remember what I said about the possibility of having a sex offender like Alfonso Rodriguez in any Day Treatment program, at almost any hospital? Yes, something very similar has already happened to me, while in a treatment program for sexual assault.

It seems obvious that parents should be warned about this possibility since President George Bush has issued an Executive Order that "every American ought to be screened for depression."

As the video on human reproduction began, I got up very quietly and left. I made my way to the Office of the Director, and complained. No investigation occurred, and I was told that the staff was "about to undergo a sensitivity training program."

Now isn't it therapists that claim to be the most empathic? Don't they claim that their refined training makes them sensitive to everyone going through any kind of traumatic experience? Isn't that why, when there's a death in the family, or a tornado rips through your neighborhood, you should rush to your doctor's office and volunteer for specialized counseling?

In the eight years since that complaint, there has been no evidence of any sensitivity training program. One would assume that before advertising for sexual assault treatment, the hospital staff would receive any needed training in sensitivity.

On the contrary. In the years since then I have been subjected to such incompetence and callousness, it would take at least fifty pages to fully describe each occurrence. I will therefore summarize.

- A resident wanted to schedule an appendectomy, and the pain was on the left side, near the rib cage. I made her call the attending physician and repeat the exam.
- Following a traffic accident in which I was the pedestrian, run down by a driver, I had to force my provider to do a thorough exam by saying, "well then doctor, maybe I ought to see a veterinarian from now on."
- Eric Dieperinck, MD, an Outpatient Psychiatrist, barred my access to my own records, because he had given me Personality 8, which is not even in the psychiatric diagnostic manual. It's illegal to bar access to records, and also illegal to falsify records, with a diagnosis no other doctor would use.
- I got no compassion as I faced cancer of the vagina. Instead, my VA OBGYN, Kamilini Das, violated my confidentiality with a witness present.

Chapter Six – The "C" Word

I was in shock in October 2001, when I got a frightening report about precancerous cells from my annual Pap smear. Most people have some kind of reaction when they are told they have cancer. A caring staff would provide all necessary information and ask if the patient had any questions. They might even attempt to answer commonly asked questions the patient might not even think to answer.

But I had already caused a fury amongst the staff at MPLS VA by choosing to discontinue treatment, after reading Toxic Psychiatry and a few other books critical of psychiatry. (See chapter for a complete discussion of all my reasons for discontinuing treatment.) Every time I went to a scheduled appointment after leaving psychotherapy, I'd be cross-examined about all my reasons for leaving treatment behind.

I never thought that decision would affect how the Woman's Comprehensive Care Clinic would deal with cancer information, but it did I got handed a stack of brochures and a promise to discuss the details at an appointment almost ten days after the initial results from the pap smear. I couldn't believe how cold the OBGYN and nursing staffs were.

During this follow up appointment, I was supposed to have a colposcopy. When I asked what that was, the nurse, Paula Newinsky, just said, "It's a routine test needed prior to treating the cells." That was it. She then told me to get dressed and left the room.

Rather than even attempting to prepare me for the possibilities I might be facing in terms of these precancerous cells, I was ordered to return to Outpatient Psychiatry for "supportive therapy, during this health crisis."

I told Dr. Das I had no intention of ever taking the psychiatric medications I was prescribed after I was raped. I told her the books and journal articles I had read prior to stopping those meds and the immediate improvement to my physical health that had occurred following my decision to try life without those meds.

The doctor then noted that I was "agitated," because of the report from the Pap smear. I paced the floor in front of my chair for less than two minutes as I was given that life changing information. I had also tossed my jacket into the chair, when I could not get any answers to my pleas for information. Isn't pacing the floor within the range of normalcy when getting an alarming report from a Pap smear?

A few tears might have even been understandable, except of course, from someone who had been treated for sexual assault recovery. And for someone who had acquired twelve psychiatric diagnoses due to that "treatment." Forever afterwards, every reaction I have to any kind of crisis in my life will be deemed a symptom of my mental illness.

So, as soon as I got home from my brief and mechanical appointment with Dr. Das, I called my nurse friend and also made an appointment at the county hospital for a second opinion. My friend came over and we had dinner together. Then we discussed all the details I didn't get from the Woman's Comprehensive Care Clinic at MPLS VA. (That clinic had been created, according to a glossy brochure to ensure that female veterans would get respectful care.)

My friend informed me that the colposcopy exam would be no more painful than a normal pelvic exam. "It's just a device that allows the doctor to photograph the area of interest."

She told me that the second opinion was a good idea since the treatment method that Dr. Das had chosen was archaic, and that I should have laser surgery instead. Dr. Das had recommended 5FU cream, which would be applied several times a day, and would burn off the bad cells. Prior to inserting this cream into my body, I would have to put rubber gloves on and smear my inner thighs with Vaseline, so that no other skin would be burned by this corrosive cream.

I was greatly relieved when Linda told me that the laser surgery was a better approach. The way the cream had to be applied sounded like a re-enactment of the rape to me. Inserting something inside of me that would burn parts of my body made me wonder if it would trigger flashbacks. Those are frightening images of the event that run through the mind like a grotesque movie.

I hadn't had any for almost six years and didn't want them back. Some rape victims can't even have a tooth pulled without having flashbacks. Any invasion of the body, for any reason, can be a trigger.

Linda thought that might be a distinct possibility and stressed that I get that second opinion, for that reason, and several others. She said that women usually recover more quickly from the laser surgery than from the cream, and seldom have the bleed through that is so common with the cream.

Now, in the weeks before getting this bad news about the Pap smear, I had begun attending a new writer's group. I'd completed the first draft of a screenplay about a female relative, who had spent part of World War II as a spy in China and Burma for the U.S. State Department.

Alma had been a positive force in my early life and I discovered that focusing on good memories and working on a future, was an excellent way to deal with both the depression and PTSD that had resulted from that rape. The president of this screenwriter's group had evaluated this script at no charge. He suggested very few changes, but they seemed both reasonable and critical for success of the script.

I discovered that it was fun to hear the dialog I had written, read by other members of the group. That's what the meeting consists of. Members take roles in the scripts of other writer's and portray the characters. This gives the writer an idea of the impact of his or her words.

I continued with this group while dealing with the ordeal of my cancer and its disrespectful treatment. It became the very best form of therapy, although most of the members did not know that I was facing cancer. It was a place to go where my skills and talents as a person would get some applause, even while Dr. Das and Paula Newinski were denying my human dignity.

That script won a consolation prize in the Writer's Digest contest for 2003. But that didn't happen until after my laser surgery.

Every step of the way, until the moment I was rolled into the operating room, was an ordeal, since even after my second opinion, which recommended the laser surgery, Dr. Das still insisted on that corrosive cream. She also demanded a list of my friends, and said she would do nothing more pertaining to my case until she got it.

One of my friends had been through cervical cancer eight years earlier and had had surgery to remove a tumor. Her surgery had taken place much later in the disease process than mine would. But she was just as outraged by my doctor's demand for that list of friendships as I was. She said she'd never heard of such a thing.

Sue has a speakerphone, so I was able to hear every bit of conversation between her and Paula Newinski the day she called the Woman's Clinic in my behalf. And when she hung up, she gave me a big hug and said, "That nurse is a bitch."

Nevertheless, I complied with the doctor's orders that I bring a friend with me to my next appointment. As we sat down in the exam room, Dr. Das shocked me by passing around copies of a letter she had Fed Ex-ed me the week before.

I asked my friend not to look at that letter and explained that it contained such confidential information that the doctor had used Fed Ex to deliver it to me, so no letter carrier could see it.

Fortunately, my friend was much more ethical than my OBGYN. He did not read the letter. Then I asked the doctor to explain why she used a courier service if she thought the information in it was so unimportant.

"I wanted a complete discussion of all treatment options which were summarized in that letter."

I then turned to John and said, "The doctor wants to use an outdated method to treat my cancer, even though another doctor would choose laser surgery."

"Can you get the laser surgery at that hospital?"

"Yes, but not for at least two months."

"Can Janet get that surgery done here any sooner?" he asked.

Dr. Das then threw the file folder from which she had taken the confidential letter on her desk so hard I thought everything in it might fall to the floor. She keyed several codes into the computer and said, "We have an operating room next week."

I remain stunned to this day that even my cancer treatment at MPLS VA had to be such an ordeal.

Had I not acquired all those inaccurate mental health diagnoses, maybe my cancer treatment might have at least respected my human dignity. But I have learned that doctors respond to mental health stigma more thoroughly than ordinary people. They know they can treat patients with psychiatric diagnoses like dogs and get away with it. They can act as they please and say that the patient imagined the whole thing.

That she fractured my rights with a witness present ought to indicate how far out of control the staff at MPLS VA really is. And now that I've publicly established that at least half of those mental health diagnoses have no basis in fact, I'm also going to say something else.

I wonder if Dr. Das was trying to provoke me into some extreme angry reaction to her fracture of my rights. She would have been overjoyed to pick up the phone and call security.

But it was John's anger and defense of my dignity that caused her to slap that file on her desk. It was his insistent questions that got that surgery for me. How sad his integrity outclassed hers.

Two weeks after recovery from my surgery was certain, I complained to the state licensing board for doctors. Doctors licensed in this state are supposed to be subject to its rules no matter what hospital might employ them.

But the Medical Practice Board did not sanction Dr. Das at all. I got an article about this adventure published in the alternate press in Minneapolis and then got it reprinted in forty papers worldwide, via a syndication service based in the Netherlands.

I then sent Dr. Das a copy and dared her to sue for libel.

Chapter Seven – Fighting Labels

Even though one of my many incorrect mental health diagnoses is paranoid personality disorder, I honestly never thought any of the nonsense I'd dealt with at MPLS VA was because I'd been singled out by any doctor or clinic. Maltreatment is so common at MPLS VA that there is no reason to think you are the only one receiving it. But using mental health diagnoses as a weapon is very effective, if the desire is to silence someone who complains when patient rights are fractured and doctors act in inhumane ways. Any time someone can be designated as paranoid, it certainly is an effective weapon.

That's what Thomas Szaszs, in Age of Anxiety has said, "once anyone is declared mentally ill, you can do anything you want to them, including torture, as long as you can claim you are doing it for their own good."[1]

The staff at MPLS VA doesn't believe it has to consider the facts of a patient's life when diagnosing mental illness, either. That's why I began a campaign to obtain public evidence to counter paranoid personality disorder and eight other ridiculous diagnoses.

Part one was the publication of my first novel in 2001, despite fourteen rejections. I found a fiction writer's group that helped me deal with the rejection common to creative endeavors. Writers present their works in progress for criticism prior to writing the final draft and seeking publication.

I am now a member in good standing with three of these groups. Two of them are fiction writer's groups and the third is a Screenwriter's group. I've written three screenplays, even though Hollywood's age bias makes it even more unlikely that they will get produced.

This has been my most vital form of therapy. I'm an equal in these groups of professional writers. If even half of my twelve diagnoses had any basis in fact, I should not be able to function in any professional group. I ought to have such difficulty in all kinds of relationships that any group not led by a therapist ought to be impossible for me.

Part two was getting Dakota Faith on KNOF radio and at www.heartlandradio.com. It will now also be included on www.springboardforthearts.com and at www.theatersycorax.com in Germany. I did all the promotion of this gospel album myself.

Part three was finding a gospel songwriting group for my remaining gospel lyrics. From this group has come an unexpected benefit – joining the band of another member to perform my own music in public. And I am not supposed to have any people skills at all, remember? Performing has been the icing on the cake, so to speak.

It never occurred to me that I might have become a target for special consideration at MPLS VA. I just think psychiatry in general has a huge inflated ego problem. This means they will treat patients as they please and then find a way to justify it.

And MPLS VA has a huge attitude problem. It has a self appointed reputation as being "the best hospital in the system." It certainly is among the newest and has all the latest equipment. Its research arm has become very well known nationwide. But it's not the equipment or reputation in academe that makes a hospital. It is how the staff carries out its responsibilities to its patients.

But according to my records, the fact that I'd complained about the fracture of my rights and made that decision to stop psychiatric medications meant that I was "distrustful."

Refusing medications is supposed to be legal. The patient should not be punished with even one new psychiatric diagnosis. I got four new ones.

I had to publicly challenge as many of them as possible in order to avoid a huge problem if I was ever raped again and my records came to court. With paranoia on my charts, I couldn't imagine how any jury might convict.

The status of my mental health records has already prevented me from filing a case. It involved the pastor in the church I'd been attending. He knew about the previous rape as I'd done some spiritual counseling with him.

One morning on my way to a temporary employment assignment, I'd locked my keys in my car. I called the temporary service to inform them about what had happened and was taken off the assignment. I then took a bus home and got my replacement key from a desk drawer. I stepped across the street and asked the pastor for a ride.

He said, "I always keep my extra in my back pocket."

Then he grabbed my butt and said, "Like this."

The Minneapolis Police said that was 5th degree sexual assault and that I'd have to prove intent in court.

In that case, my treatment records would have been subpoenaed, since the pastor knew about my rape and subsequent mental health treatment. So I didn't file. Instead I reported it to the deacons of the church. A similar situation was reported about a year later, and the pastor was retired early.

Chapter Eight – Keeping the Victim in Bondage

Jeffrey Masson, MD, has a lot to say about the power imbalance that's characteristic of psychotherapy. It's one of the major themes of Against Therapy.

People who come into treatment, whether self-referred or because of some recent trauma, come looking for answers from an "expert." There is usually some element of desperation in seeking professional help.

More and more today, parents are urged to get help when their children have difficulty in school. Not only urged, but oftentimes intimidated into initiating "treatment." This sets up a relationship between therapist and patient which parallels that of a small child to parent.

The patient is hoping that the wise doctor can somehow make the deep pain go away, or make some sense out of the confusion dominating his/her life. This grants the therapist god-like power.

And whereas the wise parent may often apologize for mistakes in parenting, few therapists will ever even admit their mistakes, even when confronted by patients. In fact, the patient is usually told that his/her perceptions are faulty.

Either that, or the patient has a deep seated distrust of authority, which naturally affects reactions to common themes in therapy.

Usually the power differential in therapy is not discussed. Any criticism of any aspect of treatment is commonly ignored. And most of the self-help books that have sold in the millions help to exaggerate the therapist as an "expert" on all aspects of life.

It pays the bills, which is one of the primary motivators for the therapist. Even more than that, a therapist with a thriving practice is applauded by colleagues and the general public as well.

But the television programs, talk radio instant solutions and the pop psychology best sellers contribute to a set of unrealistic expectations by the person seeking help.

If the practitioner could do even half of the miracles common to these books and programs, they could prevent the horrid attrition rate in their own profession. Mental health practitioners commit suicide more often than any other profession. That ought to say something to counter some of the outrageous claims for therapy. To illustrate this statement, I'll quote from several books by well known practitioners.

Now that the FDA has publicly admitted that the SSRI antidepressants can increase suicidal ideation and violence in some patients, it might seem a bit ironic to quote Listening to Prozac, by Peter Kramer MD. However, one of his case studies illustrates this doctor as god problem they all seem to have.

He tells about this young woman who grew up in an alcoholic family and took care of her siblings until she graduated from high school. This of course, automatically makes her a martyr, sacrificing most of her social life to make sure her brothers got basic care.

She unfortunately married an alcoholic and suffered bouts of physical abuse from her husband. After six months on Prozac, this wonder drug so altered her personality that, she was no longer acting "like a masochist," according to Dr. Kramer. He explains that her masochism was "grounded in her low self esteem."[1]

I'm quite sure the doctor did not tell her that he considered her a masochist. Her alcoholic mate probably blamed her for all the mayhem his drinking caused in both of their lives. Most alcoholics blame everyone except themselves.

And when her life is in shambles and she comes to the great doctor for help, from his lofty perch, he also blames her by calling her "masochist." That label is hardly nonjudgmental.

Blaming the victim is the hallmark of psychotherapy, according to Jeffrey Masson. He says, "By its very nature, psychotherapy must pretend to supply an objective and humane atmosphere to those who wish to express their deepest feelings of pain and sorrow. The tragedy is that this legitimate need is exploited, even if with good intentions, by therapists who claim to offer what has never been theirs to give."[2]

The best example of how therapists continually blame the patient is the attitude expressed by Jerome Kroll, MD in Challenge of the Borderline. People with borderline personality disorder are supposedly very manipulative and move from crisis to crisis, never able to find healthy and positive relationships. He says this compulsion for choosing dangerous relationships means that the patient could be held responsible for his/her own murder.[3] With that kind of attitude, one must hope that Dr. Kroll is never the expert witness in a murder trial.

David Healy makes this stunning statement about blaming patients for side effects. Psychiatrists blamed schizophrenia for antipsychotic-induced problems such as the chronic and disfiguring facial grimacing of tardive dyskinesia. Everyone at present blames the patient's personality for addiction, rather than the agent he is being treated with for benzodiazepine or SSRI-induced dependence.[4]

Lilly (Prozac's manufacturer) and many clinicians have spectacularly blamed depression rather than Prozac for drug-induced suicidality. This history suggests that those delivering a therapy are not the best people to bring the hazards of that therapy to light.

And a good example of how therapists exploit their patients is the claim by Joseph McMullen, in Prozac Backlash, concerning one of his patients who had acrophobia. Since Dr. McMullen believes in using antidepressants sparingly and for a very short time, his reflections about his own miraculous talents had to do with verbal therapy.

In less than a year, this patient was supposedly able to obtain a high paying job as a stock broker on the forty fifth floor of a New York skyscraper.

And even though most psychiatrists who write such books usually indicate that their case studies are composites of numerous patients, Dr. McMullen stated that he had a release to use this information. Could someone with acrophobia really take a job in a skyscraper, after only a few months with the great doctor? It sounds just like the faith healers on religious television.

This is a common problem for practitioners. Do the claims they make about the effectiveness of whatever treatment modality they are promoting, actually hold water? Jeffrey Masson says this: "Everybody should know that stepping into the office of a psychotherapist is entering a world where great harm can be done."[5]

Nevertheless, Prozac Backlash is a very good resource about side effects of this class of meds. It adds to Toxic Psychiatry, by defining some of the strange withdrawal symptoms some patients have endured. In these patients, the nervous system misfires, creating such excruciating pain that they have had to go back on their medication, and be introduced to another drug in this class before being tapered off.[6]

Lilly, the manufacturer of Prozac knew this as early as 1990, three years before Listening to Prozac was written. An internal memo read –

> The incidence of suicidal acts under Fluoxetine (Prozac) therefore purely mathematically are 5.6 times higher than the other active medication, Imipramine one of the tricylic antidepressants. It is of the greatest importance that it be determined whether there is a particular subgroup of patients who respond better to Fluoxetine than to Imipramine, so that the higher incidence of suicide attempts may be tolerable."[7]

Prozac Backlash also states that some patients on SSRIs have had some of the movement disorders common to anti-psychotics. In the late stages of some of these disorders, people move about like startled chickens.

The jerkiness can be so profound that walking becomes almost impossible. It was thought that SSRIs were free from this complication.

Yet despite the growing body of evidence that SSRIs can create many more problems than they solve, far too many psychiatrists are still sold on prescribing them. In Getting Your Life Back, The Complete Guide to Recovery from Depression, Jesse Wright MD, insists that there is no danger for physical addiction with any of these anti-depressants.[8]

Since it was published before the black box warnings were announced, Dr. Wright might claim that the facts about these meds were unknown.

But there have been more than a half dozen major lawsuits against the makers of these medications, in which addiction has been proven. The largest award was for $8.1 million in a suit in against Paxil in California in 1999. Also, the "Prozac defense," has become quite popular in murder cases, where the person exhibited no previous violent behavior. But after being on Prozac or one of its sister medications, went on a violent rampage.[9]

The makers of Luvox were sued by the parents of Eric Harris, one of the shooters in the Columbine massacre. Harris had been taking the medication for well over a year, and had been deemed "much improved" by his therapist. The drug maker did not fare well in this wrongful death lawsuit.

In the recent Red Lake Massacre, in northern Minnesota, Jeffrey Weise, the shooter, was on a large dose of Prozac. He was taking 60 milligrams per day. The usual dose for adults is half that amount. The jury is not in yet in that case. Most psychiatrists will avoid any connection between the drug and the violent act, by simply saying the "underlying mental illness," was at fault. If the drug was helping at all, there should be no underlying illness, especially if one subscribes to the original propaganda as presented in Listening to Prozac.

Dr. Kramer claimed that it was possible to use SSRIs to mold the patient's personality. He used several case studies to underline this assertion. But he also admits that he saw his patients once every two months for fifteen minutes or less. How could he claim to know anything real about any of them?

He also claimed that there was no possibility of addiction: no serious side effects. But the professional literature was full of reports of violent acts connected to Prozac. Because of that well-known potential to make things worse for patients, Germany never licensed Prozac, or any of its sister medications, which were promoted as safer. It also had some difficulty getting licensed in Britain.

Some psychiatrists still take this approach, despite the black box warnings. They are now willing to admit to some of the most obvious side effects, such as constipation, loss of interest in sex, digestive disorders, and weight gain.

This approach is to continue to use these medications and regain the patient's trust by developing ways to cope with the side effects. This ensures that the doctor's bank account will not be grossly affected by the black box warning labels, recently passed by the FDA.

In The Antidepressant Survival Program, Robert S. Haedaya, proposes diet, alternative meds, and a thorough examination, to determine if there might be some underlying condition precipitating the depression. What a unique idea: a thorough physical exam. Canadian doctors have been doing this for decades.

His program is for the sexual dysfunction common to these meds and the unhealthy weight gain. (I lost sixty pounds with little effort after stopping my Zoloft. I have also kept it off, since I no longer have compulsive eating patterns. I wonder if an excess of serotonin in the brain, interferes with hunger signals.)

I also wonder if the widespread use of these meds might be an unaddressed factor in the increased rate of obesity nationwide. The acquisition of sixty extra pounds would <u>cause</u> depression in most people. In a society that places such a profound emphasis on body image, weight gain is no minor side effect.

The cruelest part about that is that I was never told that Zoloft might be responsible for those extra seventy five pounds. Rather, I was blamed for that problem.

I was told that my compulsive eating was my way of dealing with stress. The over use of comfort foods from childhood might even be considered an addiction. I was referred to a dietician and even enrolled in an inpatient program for obesity.

In promoting his plan for those who choose to continue to take these meds, Dr. Haedaya once again demonstrates the expansive ego common to this profession. "Gradually, I came to see myself as a conductor who tuned and harmonized the various instruments within the vast orchestra of my patients' minds and bodies. Antidepressants all too frequently introduced new disharmonies, throwing other parts of the orchestra out of tune."[10]

A psychiatrist – god, who coordinates all aspects of their patient's healthcare? As mentioned before, the usual session is fifteen minutes every two months. And most of them seldom even use a stethoscope. Instead, the patient is referred to a steady stream of specialists. These meds keep the medical profession busy indeed: busy and able to keep their bank accounts in the black.

In therapy, the therapist's self esteem grows and grows. Does the patient's self esteem really grow as much as the practitioner's? Not according to Jeffrey Masson. He says the very act of seeking help means that the patient is surrendering tremendous power over their own lives. "Imbalance in power rarely leads to compassionate behavior. Yet it is just such compassionate behavior that we have been conditioned to expect from a therapist."[11]

He recommends firing your therapist and confiding in friends instead. That's what I've been doing for the last seven years. Friends sometimes gossip and that hurts, but their opinions can be challenged in court and have no effect on my medical records. Besides, I've learned the hard way that therapists can breach confidentiality as often as they desire and licensing boards do nothing real about it.

Comfort from a friend is actually much more genuine, since they are not earning $150-200/hr for their comments. And since I now have twelve diagnoses, I know that the notes on my charts conform to my "symptoms" to whatever the current diagnosis might be. Rather than using the facts of my life to find the right diagnosis, those facts have either been ignored or twisted to conform to the most current diagnosis.

And now, if I was raped, and my psychiatric records were subpoenaed by a defense attorney, no jury would convict. An assailant could now say it was consensual sex and that I had imagined the rest of it. The jury would probably agree with that statement. I cannot be grateful to psychiatry/psychology for such total character assassination.

Over the last five years, I have embarked upon a public campaign to amass evidence to refute all but three of my twelve diagnoses. It has involved temporary work in customer service, publication of the first of seven novels, and performing my own gospel music at churches and bookstores.

Why have I done this? My medical records now depict me as someone who cannot form any kind of healthy relationship. Someone who really had all these deficits could not do any of the things I've done in the last five years.

Was there any other way to challenge any of these bogus diagnoses? Not to my knowledge. The underlying dogma in psychiatry/psychology states that "denial of mental illness is proof of same." So the things I've done will be accepted in court as evidence against these many punitive diagnoses.

This kind of assault on my character should not be allowable in a free society. But as Jeffrey Masson, MD states in Against Therapy, his "profession is corrupt." It has acquired irrational power over a nation of desperate people: A nation of people who have been programmed to see themselves as victims of one sort or another.

Chapter Nine – Brain Damage?

Just prior to Dr. Dieperinck's diagnosis of Personality 8, I had obtained a copy of Toxic Psychiatry, and now understood how dangerous the psychiatric meds I'd been taking in good faith really were. I briefly summarized the contents of this important book in chapter two. Now I will go into greater detail.

Peter Breggin, MD begins this work by describing the theory behind Prozac and all it's sister medications. These meds are supposed to increase the effectiveness of one neurochemical-serotonin. Serotonin was first isolated in the muscle. The word combines two Latin words: sero, meaning blood, and tonin, meaning muscle.

One of the theses of Toxic Psychiatry is that rather than enhancing brain function over the long haul, this class of antidepressant actually causes damage to brain cells.

He also argues that clinical experience showed that suicidal ideation could increase while taking these meds. It chronicles a series of mega-law suits which have established this problem in courts. But even before these lawsuits, the potential to increase suicidal ideation was well-documented in professional journals. Dr. Breggin lists and analyzes all of these articles.

This book goes into great detail about the drug trials conducted prior to FDA approval. Research subjects who indicated any previous suicidal thoughts were excluded from tests for all these medications. The obvious question seems to me to be, how can any doctor know whether these medications will help a severe depression, if the tests did not allow for that. If you excuse someone from the tests who has a symptom you later treat with that med, you are asking for problems.

It was this book that allowed me to believe that I might leave psychotherapy behind, since the only reason I was now continuing treatment was because I was intimidated into believing that disaster would occur if I stopped these medications.

Dr. Breggin advised all readers to obtain medical supervision prior to tapering off these medications, as backlash can occur. I made several phone calls to see if there might be a doctor in Minnesota willing to provide that type of supervision. I could find no one. I wondered whether that might be because so much of the Minnesota economy is dependent upon mental health care. None of the doctors I spoke to would comment on that question.

So I tapered myself off the Zoloft and Mellaril. I had been trying to convince Dr. Dieperinck for some time that those medications were not really helping me at all. He ignored my comments. I therefore decided not to tell him that I'd stopped my meds for almost four months. I wanted to see if he could detect any changes in "affect."

It was shortly after that that he illegally barred my own access to my records. A female Korea era veteran, who had held managerial positions in the American Legion, got them for me. She had acquired a paralegal certificate, and knew everyone in Minneapolis VA hospital.

Sure enough, Dr. Dieperinck had done exactly what most therapists do when they are angry at their patients or clients – he retaliated on my medical records. I was never supposed to know about Personality 8.

I was very fortunate that in tapering off as I did, that I had no withdrawal. Antidepressants can be as addictive as valium, even though they are supposed to be safe. Just a few months after I stopped taking Zoloft, another antidepressant in that class, Paxil, lost a huge law suit in California. The drug maker was charged with fraud for denying its addictive nature.

But I had nothing but smooth sailing. Within six weeks, my fibromyalgia, diverticulosis, sleep apnea and irritable bowel syndrome were gone. And my life did not get worse. Shortly thereafter my first novel, Naked in the Parade, was published. A year and a half later, and my first gospel album has received free airplay on heartlandradio.com and soon will be included on two new websites: springboard for the arts, and theater sycorax in Munich Germany.

Now about Dakota Faith, I know nothing about musical composition, so I had to collaborate with a musician. If even half of my twelve diagnoses had any basis in fact, collaboration with anyone ought to be impossible for me. Songwriter's Market describes collaboration as one of the most difficult relationships to manage.

According to my medical records, I'm not supposed to be able to sustain any relationship: not supposed to have any people skills at all. That's precisely why I've taken several customer service jobs for various temporary services, during this period.

I'm not supposed to have any flexibility in my personality either. One who is that rigid ought to be incapable of cooperating on any creative project.

Furthermore, because I complained about that Day Hospital program in which I was the only woman, I'm supposed to "hate all men." I've been told this by several medical practitioners at MPLS VA, since then. That's absolutely ridiculous, but that's how MPLS VA attempts to defend its callous attitude.

Dakota Faith proves that I don't "hate all men," since the musician who did the arrangements and provides the vocals, is a male Vietnam veteran. He is now in assisted living, in part due to Agent Orange complications.

And what makes it even more impossible, according to those records, is the fact that my brother committed suicide about two months before I began writing all those lyrics. Even more impossible was the fact that he made that choice just three months after my first surgery for dysplasia. That's the precancerous condition that resulted in Dr. Das' fracture of my confidentiality.

I decided to try complaining to the Woman Veteran Center in Washington, D.C. I got a formal apology, but to my knowledge, the staff has yet to be disciplined with respect to that complaint. I had intended to use my Medicare benefits and stay away from MPLS VA. That formal apology encouraged me to try again.

Problems have mushroomed anyway. I could not get a refill for my diabetes med, despite being referred to a podiatrist because I am diabetic. He would not write me a new script. Instead, I was referred to pharmacy. The pharmacist referred me to Urgent Care and there I was told I'd have to wait until my next scheduled appointment with my internist. That was not to happen for sixty days.

I lost it at that point. I screamed at the patient rep. "I don't want to die, you ninny. I only have five days left of this life or death medication." He would not help me get either samples, or a temporary refill.

The next day I went to the county hospital and got the med refilled until I could see my VA doctor.

Rather than refilling this essential medication, I was sent a letter to appear before the Patient Behavior Committee. (PBC) When I called the doctor whose signature appeared at the bottom of the letter, Lori Suvalsky, MD, I was told that this committee had been in existence for seventeen years and had disciplined hundreds of veterans during that time. (Dr. Suvalsky is a psychiatrist in inpatient psychiatry, and therefore is of course, totally without bias where I'm concerned.)

When I pointed out that I would not have been alive to contact her had I not gotten my diabetes medication filled outside the VA system, she said, "that's not my concern." Of course not. All she cares about is that I was impolite with her staff as I faced an unnecessary crisis pertaining to that medication. My loss of control was not such that hospital security was called, however. Any quasi police force **has** to listen to both sides of the story.

I had a hunch that the PBC had no real legal authority over me, so I never appeared before it. I found it interesting that the PBC could not be located on any internal telephone list by the switchboard operator. I don't know of any other standing committee in the federal service without a receptionist, or at least a voice mail. Federal agencies love to spend tax dollars. Such a committee, if it were real, would have more staff than necessary and lots of requisitions for equipment deemed necessary to carry out its mission.

By that time I had received that formal letter of apology from my advocate at the Woman Veteran Center in Washington, D.C. And when I mentioned to Dr. Suvalsky that Meri Mallard had already had a conversation with the coordinator of the Woman's Comprehensive Care Clinic, she groaned. I suggested that my case be referred to Ms. Mallard. Dr. Suvalsky did not like that at all.

I have requested the by laws and all agendas that do not mention any other veteran disciplined by this committee. If it really has been in existence for seventeen years, there ought to be a stack of agendas of board meetings. Six months have passed since I requested this information from Dr. Suvalsky. In a

Janet Saugstad

Freedom of Information Act letter, I asked for the paper trail on this committee: the first typewriter or computer ever ordered, the first file cabinet and box of paper clips, and one item for each fiscal year it's been in existence. None of these documents exist. Any committee that regularly disciplines veterans ought to have a safe way of dealing with the documents pertaining to any case. Not having its own file cabinet makes that impossible.

Since then, I lost my glucose meter and went to three different clinics before being told it would not be replaced. Again, the county hospital replaced it for me, no problem.

But that same hospital fractured my patient, human and civil rights in January, 2003. That's the topic for chapter nine.

Chapter Ten – Take Care, Sweetie

As a society, over the past thirty-five years, we have been bombarded with psychobabble. Books like Listening to Prozac, which deliberately present only one side of the story, have proliferated. They laud the medications and present the mental health practitioner as capable of solving almost any problem known to humankind.

Since we all have such a deep need to believe that someone really cares when life makes no sense, the psychiatric industry in the United States, is a multibillion-dollar enterprise. Their propaganda has been much more effective than anything Joseph Goebbels ever dreamed up. He was the Nazi official that managed that regime's publicity campaign. He developed "the big lie" theory.

It's that theory that has worked so well in this thirty-five year campaign by American psychiatry. When treatment methods in state hospitals prior to the advent of Thorazine and the first antidepressants are analyzed, it is somewhat justifiable to say that the latest drugs are somewhat safer.

But that is not what has been said in public. And the public doesn't know that the medical profession is comparing oranges to apples, because prior to the publication of Toxic Psychiatry, and Against Therapy, the full extent of patient agony in treatment centers was unknown.

But if you don't know something about previous therapies, you don't understand why doctors can still claim some degree of safety even after the black box warnings were passed.

Psychiatry has a long history of sadism in this country. It's built into the fabric of this pseudo-science. The medical director of our first asylum was a good example of the way in which doctors have always acted toward their mentally ill patients. Benjamin Rush was a signer of the Constitution, and a prominent doctor during the early years of our democracy. But though he signed off on political freedom, he did not hesitate to sell a young female patient into white slavery when her father was incapable of paying her bill for treatment.

As mentioned in a previous chapter, physical abuse of patients has been, and still remains quite common in inpatient facilities. All kinds of actions destructive of human dignity can occur when doctors "need to establish structure" on the ward. Assault is seldom reported unless the patient's life is involved.

And in the case of Electro Convulsive Therapy (ECT) and Insulin Shock Therapy (IST), the patient's life often was in jeopardy. Both of these very sadistic treatments were in common use prior to the discovery of the first antidepressants and Thorazine.

ECT is still used quite frequently and doctors claim it's much more humane than it was even three decades ago. Now patients are anesthetized and strapped down, so they don't fracture their spine while writhing about during seizures.

Watching a friend or loved one having a seizure would cause most people to take them to the nearest emergency room, to allay further problems. But seizure disorder is somehow considered medicinal for people who have major depression or Bipolar disorder.

Much has been written and filmed about ECT. It's insulin shock therapy I'm most interested in for this chapter. For this so-called therapy, large dosages of insulin were administered and the patient went into diabetic shock, while the medical staff stood around and took notes.

What was therapeutic about such a bestial practice?

It was thought that the massive seizures that developed during this form of treatment would interrupt the brain waves causing whatever mental illness was being treated. It was administered for major depressions, manic depression and schizophrenia.

In Toxic Psychiatry, Dr. Breggin goes into great detail explaining the patient's anguish during one of these treatments. Each patient could be expected to live through this torture several times each month, while undergoing standard treatment in a state hospital.

Patients would writhe about on the floor and act like wild animals and doctors and nurses would stand around and observe. The patient would beg and scream for water as abject thirst overtook them. But the staff would not intervene to stop this torture until the patient became unconscious, at which time glucose would be administered.

How can any doctor or any human being, for that matter, stand around and observe such horrid pain and suffering and refuse to intervene with a simple solution, which would immediately alleviate that agony?

Therapists will tell you that the training they undergo makes them even more sensitive to human suffering than those not in the profession, but how can that possibly be true? Isn't it an inborn human characteristic to try to alleviate suffering?

Doctors must actually learn how to suppress that natural instinct in order to do some of the things they do. Just reading about insulin shock therapy made me want to vomit. Little did I know that I would live through something very similar to it in January of 2003.

In 1995, I was first diagnosed with diabetes. That was one inherited illness I never thought I'd have to worry about. No one in the four generations I knew about in my family had ever had that disease. I subsequently learned from the Prozac survivor's support network, (www.pssg.com) that diabetes 2 is a common malady in people who have been treated with Prozac. On their website it's listed as a side effect, though no medical doctor will confirm this. Instead, doctors claim diabetes 2 has a strong correlation to obesity.

Both of my grandmothers were overweight and did not have diabetes. My maternal grandmother was huge: barely five feet tall and never under two hundred twenty pounds since the day I was born. My paternal grandmother was taller and at least fifty pounds lighter. They both lived into their nineties and died of natural causes, despite a diet rich in saturated fats and sweets. Both also lived with second hand smoke for part of their lives.

None of the men in the family had ever had diabetes. So I was completely surprised when I went to the doctor and asked to be tested for it. I had become a compulsive eater while taking Zoloft. I was told that was also related to the rape. Although my weight gain was actually a side effect of the med, I was blamed for it.

When medical personnel control all information on physical illnesses, the patient usually only gets part of the truth.

The sixty pounds I'd gained came off easily when I stopped taking Zoloft.

Now there's one doctor willing to admit that one of the major side effects of SSRIs is obesity. But of course, Dr. Haedaya in The Antidepressant Survival Program has the ideal solution for it. Stay on the antidepressant and change the diet and take more pills to counter the effects of your original med. This is good medicine?

And while I was faithfully taking Zoloft and being told it was perfectly safe, I was also being lectured about my weight. I was referred to a dietitian and participated in a program for obesity. I was a beanpole compared to everyone else in that program.

But of course I felt bad that I couldn't get my appetite under control. And my mental health case manager lied and said, "Some people use alcohol and street drugs after rape. Your addiction of choice is food."

But in August of 1995, I believed everything my medical providers told me about what was happening to my health, even when I was blamed for the side effects I was experiencing. And despite the fact that I now supposedly had three forms of depression and two personality disorders, I chose to see this devastating diagnosis of diabetes 2 as a challenge. That ought to have been impossible according to my medical records.

I did change my diet. I got all the sugar out of it as quickly as possible. I walked whenever my fibromyalgia would allow me to. As a result of this program, I lost twenty pounds in three months and kept it off.

I lost the remaining poundage when I stopped my meds in 1999. As a result, I had no major complications between 1995 and 2003. But I was still taking my diabetes med on the morning of January 13, 2002, when I walked a mile to a restaurant for a light breakfast.

As I finished my meal, I began hearing a voice telling me to do all kinds of strange things. Never in my life had I had any kind of psychotic episode before. I had never had any problems with the police either except the cop who interrogated me six times before arresting my rapist. But within fifteen minutes, the police were called and I was taken to Hennepin County Medical Center (HCMC).

HCMC is not the closest hospital to that restaurant. It's easily a ten-mile drive, through thick city traffic from where I was, but it is a trauma one center.

Long before we got even halfway there, I passed out in the back seat of the police cruiser. I was in and out of consciousness for two and a half days.

I remember coming to several times during my period in the emergency department and begging for food. One time I had to beg to be allowed to go to the ladies room. Two security guards escorted me and when I was finished, they threw me back into a four point restraint so hard that I hit my head on the wall near the left side of that contraption. It raised a lump the size of a quail egg within a few seconds. Then I passed out again.

I was admitted unconscious to the psychiatric ward. Unconscious. That ought to be illegal, since I was incapable of signing admission forms and not court ordered.

The first three days I was there, my blood sugar was only 48 in the morning. For most diabetics sixty is dangerous. At 48, I should have been on the road to a coma, but I was coherent.

Debra Betow, MD, the psychiatrist assigned to my case asked if I was hearing voices. I said I had heard a voice, but I was okay now. She wanted to know all the details of what the voice had said. I decided to keep that information secret. That bothered her, but I held my ground.

I was trying to figure out why I was on the ward. I remembered a little of the trip to the hospital and one time when I begged to be allowed to go home and feed my cat.

The security guard said my cat would be okay.

I said, "She didn't have much food in her dish. Please let me call a friend if I'm going to be here for a while."

That's what I was thinking about while the doctor was trying to get information about the weird voice that was no longer bothering me. Most people don't experience a psychotic episode this way. It might take three weeks before any medication will affect hallucinations. That much I knew by being around people in that kind of crisis. So I asked for phone privileges and called a friend to feed Bujeau.

The doctor prescribed Seroquel and I agreed to it as I really did think maybe the voice might come back as she claimed.

I was a little frightened. I mainly wasn't sure what was going on. Nothing was clear to me about anything that had happened.

Now I know that psychotic like symptoms are quite common when blood sugar drops suddenly. That's supposed to be common knowledge among medical personnel. But they get paid much more by Medicare by admitting patients to a psychiatric unit and filling them full of anti-psychotics, instead of a glucose drip in the arm.

I didn't know about those psychotic like symptoms until I spoke to my nurse friend. Her mother-in-law has diabetes and often has trouble staying in reality. Linda carries candy with her for her mother-in-law.

There's no real reason I should be alive to write this book today. If I was coherent with a blood sugar of only 48, I have to wonder what it was when I was struggling with consciousness. I also wonder how close to a diabetic coma I might have been, while the staff stood around and took notes.

I took the Seroquel while on that ward. But when she wanted to add another antipsychotic, I decided to try giving twelve-hour notice instead. That means that you are telling the doctor to either discharge you, or get a court order. I reasoned that since the voice had not returned and since I had been no problem to the staff or other patients, she would have a hard time convincing a court that I had a permanent psychosis.

I really didn't understand that it was hypoglycemia at that point. All I knew was that whatever had happened, my psychotic symptoms had disappeared. Then the nursing staff tried to convince me to reconsider my twelve-hour notice. One by one they came to talk to me, just in case it was a personality clash with the nurse assigned to my case.

Then I knew something was up. Dr. Betow had no problem throwing her weight around in court. She took three other patients to court in the week I was there. If she could have sustained Bi-Polar disorder with psychotic features in court, she would not have hesitated for ten seconds.

I had really become a thorn in their sides also. Every time they started a conversation in the common area, where other patients could listen in, I responded by discussing medication side effects only.

I did that in part, because there were several conference rooms to which I might have been escorted if they cared at all about my confidentiality. Dr. Betow proudly admitted that she had called the Veteran's Administration about my most recent hospitalization.

In this state, a patient's signature is required on a release form for such information, but once again, I was unconscious when she called the VA for that information and therefore could not sign such a release.

The nursing staff did not like discussing side effects of medications every time they wanted information, but I was not going to violate my own patient rights by discussing personal matters in any part of that facility so long as anyone could listen in. It was causing frustration for them so if they could have silenced me by a court appearance...

One of the other patients came and threw her arms around me on the day of discharge and said she was glad I was only angry at the staff, not her.

I smiled and said, "I haven't taken any of these meds in seven years, and my life has gotten better, not worse. I'm not very popular with medical people."

"Thanks for making the nurses tell us the truth about our drugs," she said.

"Good luck," I said. Then I left.

As soon as I got to the public library, I looked up Seroquel in the Physician's Desk Reference (PDR). I was horrified. There's a two page warning about vascular shock when prescribing Seroquel, yet Dr. Betow had also prescribed a blood pressure med while I was on the psychiatric unit. I had never had hypertension before.

It also has a warning about strenuous exercise while taking Seroquel. Yet the only class I was allowed to go to off the ward was an exercise class in the weight room, for heaven's sake.

Then I remembered my conversation with the other patient about not being popular with the medical staff, because my life got better without their wonder drugs. I think that's another reason for my twelve diagnoses. It's axiomatic that the person's mental and physical health declines without those meds, so even though my health improved, on my charts, it got worse.

"Given the detrimental effects of hypoglycemia on brain function, emotional symptoms have been attributed to hypoglycemia by some observers, including some physicians." 1.

Some diabetics suffer untold numbers of episodes of asymptomatic hypoglycemia and an average of two episodes of symptomatic hypoglycemia per week. At a minimum, 25% suffer an episode of severe, at least temporarily disabling hypoglycemia, often with seizure or coma, in a given year. In addition, about 4% of deaths of diabetes have been attributed to hypoglycemia."[1]

Still, it took almost two weeks for me to get the results, which were normal. I still can't believe how cruelly I've been treated at every turn, medically.

Chapter Eleven – Shoot the Messenger

I was stunned after reading all the information pertaining to Seroquel in the PDR. I had asked to see the PDR on the ward. Dr. Betow brought me one that she said was four years old. Its spine was duct taped and I wasn't sure one that old would have the information I needed. So I found a newer one at the public library after discharge.

It had a two-page warning about Seroquel's tendency to cause vascular shock. That was without any blood pressure medication. Dr. Betow ordered a blood pressure medication while I was in her care. So, not only did she ignore the warning about that tendency toward vascular shock, by ordering the blood pressure medication, she increased the risk already inherent in Seroquel. I couldn't believe any doctor could deliberately violate such an extensive warning about blood pressure. But then I still can't believe that any doctor could do what my OBGYN at the VA did, while I was facing cancer.

Someone with the means to hire the expert witnesses needed to fund a malpractice suit might expect to be treated with more respect than I. Doctors know that Medicare patients don't have the financial resources to respond to fractures of their human and patient rights.

Also all the punitive mental health diagnoses on my records would make any complaint to the licensing boards suspect. That's one good reason for a therapist who has been disciplined to assign a new diagnosis. It ensures that this patient will receive even less respect for her rights and a lower quality of medical care, each time she complains.

But putting my life in jeopardy by violating the warnings about vascular shock surely wouldn't go unnoticed by either the Medical Director of the hospital or the Medical Practice Board, would it? Despite all that had already happened denying me any semblance of justice for the multiple fractures of my patient rights, I had to believe that something would be done.

My blood pressure had never been unstable for more than three days at a time. As I began menopause, it was elevated for three days, but moderated as soon as my body adapted to that change. Seroquel is supposed to be one of the safest anti-psychotics, but it is known to cause fluctuations in blood pressure. That is its major flaw, that and its tendency for movement disorders. No anti-psychotic is free from that, and neither are the SSRIs, according to Joseph McMullen in Prozac Backlash.

While in the hospital, I was most often orthostatic in the morning, until ten a.m. So much so in fact, that getting out of a chair meant holding on to a table for support. Walking down the hallway required hanging on to a handrail.

After eight years, most diabetics have problems with their vascular, cardiac, or renal systems. My most recent cardiac stress test had been normal. But these are risks that are supposed to be considered when choosing a medication.

Most anti-psychotics can affect heart rhythm. My father died at age 40 of a coronary, and one of my brothers also had a heart attack, so my risks for cardiac and vascular difficulties were very high.

I did not ask that question in the complaint I filed shortly after discharge. I sent an immediate four page complaint to Michael Belzer, the Medical Director of HCMC. I also sent that complaint to Mary Ellen Otremba, a state representative who sits on two mental health committees. We have lots of committees and agencies that are supposed to provide oversight of the mental health system, but usually they just explain why the patients' rights have been abused. The representatives don't take any corrective action for the client, unless sexual or physical assault has been involved.

In a brief cover letter I asked that Ms. Otremba consider a subpoena for the glucose meters on the ward while they would still show the extremely low blood sugar on admission. I did this because I've seen how therapists often cover up when criticized for their lack of ethics. But Ms. Otremba did not even investigate.

Neither did Dr. Belzer. Therefore all that my complaint accomplished was a complete sanitation of my medical records.

That meant that none of the low blood sugar readings were available when I contacted the Medical Practice Board.

Now I know that complaining to the licensing board for doctors who practice in Minnesota is a waste of time and postage. Even though Dr. Betow fractured my rights numerous times, and violated the FDA warnings about vascular shock, nothing was done. The board contacted her and that's all.

I was told when I reported Eric Dieperinck for that psychiatric diagnosis of Personality 8, that "doctors have discretion in the way they respond to the rules that govern them."

That would seem to violate the Constitution, since all people are supposed to be equal in the eyes of the law. Why even have laws and rules governing medical conduct if doctors can decide, willy-nilly, when to violate them.

On that diagnosis, the American Psychiatric Association could not give me a description of Personality 8. If it's a valid diagnosis, the APA's expert on the diagnostic manual (DSM4R) ought to have been able to find a description for me. It was Wendy Squirrel who responded to my email request for information.

Since the board thinks doctors can do as they please, I should not be surprised that Dr. Betow was not disciplined. But her cover up can be proven.

She claims that one of the reasons for my hospitalization was a delayed reaction to my brother's suicide. But we could not have had even one conversation about his death, because he was still alive while I was on the ward illegally.

His body was not found until almost two weeks after my AMA discharge. On the day I was informed that he had killed himself, February 6, 2002, I had a job interview at The Volleyball Warehouse in Burnsville, MN.

Though I was in deep shock, I kept that appointment. The job was in Customer Service, and even despite this deep trauma, I came in third. There were only two slots available, so I wasn't hired.

Apparently that severe psychosis that Dr. Betow still insists I have is very fleeting. On the day his body was found, I was able to perform fairly well in a high stress interview for a customer service position. That in no way minimizes the impact of his death. It is now two years later and at times, it still hurts.

Since Dr. Betow and I could never have had a conversation about his death, due to its timing, how did she find out about it? After my experience with my VA OBGYN's lack of respect for my confidentiality, I decided to use my Medicare benefits for medical care at one of the branch clinics of HCMC.

I had to see this doctor just after Jerry's funeral as I had a vaginitis, and reported his suicide. It is part of my medical history. Richard Reif, MD wanted to put me on an SSRI as I faced this trauma, but I said no. I also said no to counseling. Why should I be honest about my feelings on any subject when my records have been so stained by so many unethical and dishonest therapists?

I then told him about my hospitalization and Dr. Betow's prescription of blood pressure meds and Seroquel. He took me off the blood pressure med, but recorded hypertension in my record anyway. I also now am supposed to have gerd, though I have no gastric problems at all. There are two other stress-related illnesses on my chart that I don't have. Refusing psychiatric medications means that you are supposed to have more problems with stress related illnesses. So whether you do or not, your records will state that you do.

Chapter Twelve – The Ground Glass Ceiling

Shortly after obtaining social security disability, it became clear that a subsistence income would never allow me to heal from that rape. As long as I was just making it month to month, there would be some form of depression with which to cope. Financial stress is a major cause of divorce and one of the reasons why depression is common after divorce.

Early in the twentieth century, the social work profession was actually created by some Bostonian women who wanted to help poor people in that city. Despite their wealth, they understood that poverty created despair. So they invested some of their money in assisting a few poor families in the run down tenements with basic necessities. This stimulated hope.

During the Great Depression, President Franklin Delano Roosevelt developed numerous work programs under the New Deal, to get people moving on their lives again. Margaret Bourke White's stunning black and white photos of the unemployed of that era still are the best depictions of the hopelessness fueled by poverty.

But all of that is forgotten in the mental health system. Self-sufficiency is not on the agenda of workshops presented by mental health practitioners in the system. Instead, everyone lives in fear of losing their benefits.

I had an unusual motivator in wanting to have public evidence with which to challenge my many diagnoses. Of course, I couldn't say that as I approached Rehabilitation Services for funding for a commonly used desktop program in journalism. To work as a reporter or editor, it is necessary to have this software knowledge. I thought that the temporary work would establish some marketable skills and computer knowledge. I was really hopeful that I might get off social security and find a form of medical insurance less destructive to my rights than that provided by the Veteran's Administration.

I was given a thorough evaluation: typing, aptitude tests, dexterity suited for factory work, IQ, math and spelling. The testing took almost three months and my social worker assured me that I would be referred to a business council affiliated with this program as soon as the tests were analyzed.

That never happened. I never was referred to any possible networking council. Although I scored well in all but the factory tests, an evaluator said I was not capable of writing a simple sentence.

That meant that no funding would be allowed for the essential software training to permit me to return to my journalism career. There was no way I could fund it myself. There was no way I could go into debt with student loans either. This means that my college degree in journalism was of no value to a state-funded agency, yet it would be at a temporary work agency.

Even though my IQ test showed me near the genius range, the overall tests showed that I was capable only of janitorial or sheltered workshop. Sheltered workshop for someone with a college degree and an IQ near the genius range? Most of the workers employed in such programs are developmentally disabled.

Their other option: janitorial was obviously designed to assist another social services program. At that time, this agency was training people for jobs as janitors. It was therefore necessary to refer as many disabled people to this "empowerment" agency as possible. But due to my arthritis and fibromyalgia, I could only lift 10 pounds. How I was supposed to do a physically demanding job like janitor, I don't know. But in this system, people quickly become important only as sources of income.

I really thought the recent clerical temp jobs might have some bearing on my employment possibilities. I never expected my education would have no bearing on my future. But that's what experts in this field do. They ignore things that employers look at when the mental health records are kept confidential.

I asked my social worker how someone with an IQ in the genius range could be expected to work in a sheltered workshop.

I said, "Not only have you destroyed my education in one swift motion, you have challenged your own tests pertaining to my intelligence."

He indicated that like it or not, the State of Minnesota would not fund any other options.

The next day, I found another temporary service, in part to retake employment tests. I scored in the 90th percentile. I got a six-week assignment in customer service.

Then I began writing my first novel, using a computer at the local library. I'd never written fiction before, but I decided I would now do so just to challenge the Rehab Services evaluator, who said I couldn't write a simple sentence. Three years later, Naked in the Parade was published and is still available at Amazon.com.

That customer service job was for a retail catalog company during the Christmas rush. That's the busiest time of the year. Retail outlets depend on sales during this time of year to keep their company profitable.

I was still taking my meds at this time and didn't know that fibromyalgia was connected to SSRIs. And in order to cope with the increased pain from fibro, I had to purchase a chemical pack that could be warmed in a microwave.

It had a cotton sleeve and Velcro fastener, which could be adjusted for wearing around the neck or knee. In a rush one day, I forgot to remove it from this sleeve when I put it in the microwave. I left the snack bar long enough to use the ladies room and when I returned, smoke was pouring from the microwave.

A supervisor was standing near the microwave and asked if I knew its chemical composition as the label had melted. I said no but told him where I'd bought it. That allowed him to learn what they needed to know.

The building was evacuated for half an hour. I expected that would end the assignment for the temporary service, but since I was honest about it, I got the benefit of the doubt. I certainly had gotten nothing like that at Rehabilitation Services or MPLS VA. I completed my assignment and had a nice Christmas.

To be able to keep any customer service job longer than three days ought to have been impossible, according to one of the diagnoses on my chart: paranoid personality disorder.

Remember, I finished the six week assignment and exceeded sales quota every week I was there. Customer service is supposed to be the most stressful job in the world. No one with even an ounce of paranoia in their personality could do such a job. Not only did this job serve to challenge the above diagnosis, it was far less aggravating to my fibromyalgia than the janitorial position Rehabilitation Services would have funded for me.

Therapists are dedicated to helping people in abusive relationships to get to safety and leave. To identify such relationships early, one is taught all of the signs of control. If your partner insists upon choosing your friends, the clothes you wear, when you come and go, that's called control.

But what do therapists do? Masson sees extreme control in therapy. He was not necessarily referring to government funded treatment when he stated that in Against Therapy.

But the level of control in therapy is even greater in the mental health system, where self-sufficiency risks a loss of healthcare benefits and food for the client. Social Security and Medicare also pays the wages for all types of therapists, nurses and auxiliary personnel. Providing real self-sufficiency means a loss of income for all of these professionals. That's why it is here that the therapist becomes the expert on every aspect of the patients' life.

The evaluator who said I was incapable of writing a simple sentence, which was why the funding I wanted was denied, did not need any kind of writing skills herself. She did not need to have ever corrected one English paper, or ever had a by-line in any kind of print or broadcast media. That means that the only way for me to challenge that absolute statement was to get published as a freelancer.

I objected to the willy-nilly assault on my college education and complained to the Commissioner of Rehabilitation Services but no investigation resulted. Same song, different verse. I got more sympathy when I wanted justice.

But justice is an alien concept in government funded therapy. Complaining to any authority over any aspect of the mental health system is like screaming into a wind tunnel.

Those who are supposed to provide oversight get paid the same salary whether they investigate complaints or not. So it's usually not.

It took almost three years to get Naked in the Parade published. It went through fourteen rejections before publication. Upon publication, I sent a copy to the Commissioner, with a short cover letter. Again, nothing was done.

When I asked, during that call, whether my claim would now be investigated, I was told that was not possible, but if I still wanted "help," I could re-open my claim for services. The thought that maybe the evaluator should be reprimanded, never crossed the Commissioner's mind.

I sent a formal letter of complaint to the governor stating that I wasn't ever supposed to have a professional resume again, but agree to bottom level jobs with no future. I pointed out in that letter that when I went to a temporary service, my bachelor's degree was acknowledged. I was paid the same as anyone else with similar credentials and experience. That's why I wanted that software program. No one from the governor's office ever called to acknowledge receipt of that complaint.

Vocational Rehabilitation through the Veteran's Administration was equally disrespectful of my office skills. I was assigned to a boring file job in an area of the hospital where few patients would ever come. I spent three hours a day reattaching patient notes to their charts. A similar job in the federal civil service would have paid at least $6.50/hr. I was paid $1.50/hr.

My point is I had computer skills, which were ignored. So was the temporary work in customer service. So was my education, once again. Temporary agencies are not allowed to discriminate. Apparently vocational rehabilitation is somehow above the laws.

But it's also very interesting that hiring agents at temporary services could not detect my severe mental illnesses. Most of them are very obvious.

So, once again, I quit that filing job in MPLS VA, and began a data entry job for a law firm – again, a temporary job. But again, my skills were honored.

I can speak to my own experience only, but the empowerment programs as I've encountered them are not about increasing the patient's self esteem, but the practitioner's. The person supervising these programs gets a line on their resume and has greater potential for promotion, regardless of how the client is employed. I could either do a bottom level job like janitorial or be a file clerk forever, despite my education and very recent verifiable skills.

After the data entry assignment was complete, I signed on to go to Vinland, a three week program for veterans seeking employment. Vinland is located on Independence Lake, about ten miles from downtown Minneapolis. In those three weeks, the veteran is supposed to develop and implement an employment search program.

It turned out to be a Day Treatment program disguised as an employment program. Again, another battery of tests was done, with the same predictable results. I raised a few eyebrows by refusing to do Tai-chi while I was there. Though it is a popular exercise program, it is often also a prelude to prayer in Buddhist countries.

I also had arthritis in both knees, and it was very painful for me to stand for more than a few minutes. No church has ever forced me to stand for any reason. When everyone else stands to sing sacred music during a worship service, I'm allowed to remain seated. The physical therapist ignored my arthritis and the doctor's comments pertaining to standing and not lifting more than 10 pounds, when she okayed Tai-chi for me.

I knew that Tai-Chi is a Buddhist ceremony because I had lived in Japan for three and a half years while an Officer's Wife. In trying to coerce me into doing Tai-Chi, the social worker assigned to my case, tried to imply that I was bigoted against Buddhists. She proudly claimed that she was pleased that the Dalai Lama had a speaking engagement at the Target Center, and she had some free tickets to hand out. Would I like to go?

I then told her that while I lived in Japan, I had several good friends who were Buddhists and several who were Shintoist. I said I'd even climbed inside a statue of Buddha in Kamakura to look out on the town through the eye of the statue. But as a Christian, I was not going to perform any religious ceremony aside from my own.

I was not allowed to wear a cross around my neck, or read a Bible in the common area, as there must be separation of church and state, so I wasn't going to do some other religious ritual. I was also encouraged to walk a maze on the hill behind the building. I pointed out that mazes like the one they wanted me to walk were invented by the Druids and therefore part of a pagan religion.

The staff person just looked at me for about two minutes before throwing up her hands and moving toward the building. I couldn't help myself. I said, "Well, if I can't wear a cross because it violates separation of church and state, then I shouldn't be forced to walk a Druid maze. They also worshipped trees. Is that on tomorrow's agenda, by any chance?" That may well have gotten me a new mental health diagnosis. But that social worker had never heard of the Druids.

I left Vinland a week ahead of time, as I decided once again that temporary work would be better. I'd broken one of the rules of the program. No one was supposed to use the computer to search for jobs until the last week of the program. I'd been sending resumes on the sly, after supper, while getting my email, which was allowed.

But I did a dozen watercolors while there and that very simple thing got me the most interesting job offer I've ever had. I never studied visual arts. Nonetheless, I'd found the employment bulletin board at Minneapolis College of Art (MCAD) and Design to have the most intriguing ads for jobs.

Shortly after returning from Vinland, I found a blurb for caricaturist on the MCAD board. It was for a summer job at a resort in Michigan. It didn't require any experience as a caricaturist. I met the prospective employer at a Denny's restaurant and he looked at my portfolio of watercolors and pencil sketches and offered me a job. It was for ten weeks only, which would have tossed me off of social security and at the end of it I'd have had to look for another job right away.

My self esteem was greatly improved by a real professional evaluation, of a skill for which I'd had no post secondary training. Both rehabilitation programs had ignored my education and inborn skills and only considered my disability. Their evaluation was for a job that would have bored me silly, with no chance for advancement. That sounded like a form of slavery to me.

I learned that ordinary people are far less likely to discriminate against the disabled than those who are paid to serve them. Therapists have a very narrow concept of what their clients can do. Of course, anyone who successfully returns to self-sufficiency is no longer a source of income.

And pertaining to the coercion I felt about quasi-religious practices at Vinland, I did contact a well-known far right lawyer who's famous for defending the rights of Christians. He was interested in my case. But I decided that was a fight that would drag out and not benefit me much in the end. I might have become a poster child and been much worse off after the dust had settled.

That was about five years ago, and that's the only lawyer that has ever considered suing the Veteran's Administration.

I approached several malpractice attorneys after Dr. Dieperinck's Personality 8 diagnosis, and could get no help at all. I didn't have the expert witness fees needed for malpractice. But most attorneys don't want to take cases for poor people, as the opposition will pile on the paperwork and overload their paralegals.

Veterans are trained to say, "oh well, you can't fight city hall" and so the staff continues to violate veteran's rights.

Chapter Thirteen – Honesty is Such a Lonely Word

I didn't want to have to expose myself by writing this. It is a risky thing to say that most of the therapists that earn their living through our U.S. government are the meanest and most callous of people. I'd like to believe that there might be some therapists who might actually respect the rules that are supposed to make therapy the safest relationship on the planet.

That's what is drilled into us in all our public media. It's such a part of our lives now, that whenever anything goes wrong in any relationship, we analyze each other with the terms therapists use without even having a full understanding of the meanings of those terms.

From my experience, there is no real oversight on therapy. Masson seems to agree with this conclusion. He says people are much safer with friends.[1] Most of the tenets of the ethical codes the licensing boards are supposed to enforce are just common courtesy. It ought to be so inborn, it doesn't need writing down. That's of course, if they truly cared. But they are basically strangers. The insight they are supposed to provide for the patient is seldom part of their internal domain.

Confronting a therapist is like when you're a parent of small children and something of sentimental or monetary value gets broken. Your questions about who did it seldom reveal the truth. In a way it's worse than that scenario. My experience, unfortunately, has been that if you say I caught you with your hand in the cookie jar, the response will be, "I don't see a cookie jar, and my hand has been on the desk all this time. It's your perception that my hand was in the cookie jar."

And since that is what you take to the licensing boards, hoping that no one else will have the same experience as you had, the boards can slap wrists in complete confidence that the patient has no further recourse. After all, some action was taken.

And unless the patient follows through and reads their own chart, they'll never know that complaining actually made things worse. Some of these twelve diagnoses I received have got to be to ensure that any further complaints will have no merit.

The fact that I was considered not worthy of the common courtesy that is the fabric of the codes of ethics, is what hurts the most. It's the thread that unites all my useless complaints about the numerous deep violations of my trust. To say that I actually got much more justice by prosecuting my neighbor for rape, makes this whole experience a living nightmare.

And for someone who advertises themselves as experts in all kinds of human relationships to be incapable of any real respect for the patients that pay the bills for their lavish lifestyles, reminds me of Jesus' comments to the Pharisees: Oh thou hypocrite. (That was a very long speech that left segments of the ruling class exposed and bleeding. I wonder if the common folk applauded as the Pharisees could think of no verbal response.)

I think it's an apt comparison in other ways too. Therapists wear halos in American society. In an age when everything is done in twenty-second sound bites, this is not hard to understand. People don't take the time to think about most of the claims made by therapists. As soon as something is backed by statistics or some "scientific" research, we automatically assume that it must be true.

America fully accepted all of the statements made by Masters and Johnson about what constitutes normal sexual attitudes and activities. For almost thirty years, their theories went unchallenged. Their concepts became bedrock in the field of psychotherapy.

And when they retired, they admitted that most of their research had been fabricated. While they were in practice, no other therapist questioned any of the methodology or conclusions they made. Even after this confession of fraud, no attempt was made to correct the assumptions they made, or take their licenses. All of their books on the subject are still available. No one seems to have heard that it was all a lie.

In Talking Back to Prozac, Peter Breggin, MD goes into great detail about how statistics can be made to imply almost anything.[2] He shoes how statistics were deliberately manipulated by the drug companies when seeking approval for SSRIs. Making money seems to have been more important than public health.

The FDA knew how deceitful those results were from the beginning of the Prozac revolution. Not only were the test subjects who admitted to even one suicidal thought excused from the studies, but the method of counting participants was deceitful. Being dismissed from the trials for any reason did not mean elimination from the total study.

Therefore, saying that thousands of people participated can't be supported unless the percentage of dismissed parties is mentioned. That this is the state of science today should be troubling. I wonder if that might be why it seems like one study shows all of the reasons why you should not eat butter and another shows just the opposite.

The lack of honesty in these drug trials and the unavailability of any real justice when ethical codes are violated make me wonder what therapy is really founded on. It claims to be about helping people find the truth about themselves and their relationships in order to make necessary changes, but it's clear that therapists can't live by their own suggestions.

Greed was a factor in the Prozac revolution as it is in psychotherapy. Listening to Prozac and all of the similar books that followed, only told one side of the story. That our public media, during this period, didn't ask some hard questions seems an outrage in retrospect. But the truth about most medical reporting is that most of it is just rewritten public relations packets from drug manufacturers. In depth analysis of obscure medical and scientific journals is rare.

The information on the dangerousness of this class of antidepressants was available but required lots of research, and it's much easier to rewrite than dig for the truth. This does not excuse the flood of one-sided books that lauded these medications.

One has to ask whether a psychiatrist who builds his or her practice by focusing on "successful" patients only, is ever the best judge of the effectiveness of the medications that provide his/her substantial income.

When it comes to depression, there have been many success stories, long before these medications or therapies existed. Thomas Jefferson is just one example. He developed a deep depression just after Gen. Cornwallis overran Williamsburg and sent him into exile in the Shenandoah Valley.

It was two years before he could be convinced to rejoin the leaders of the Revolutionary War. But some of his most interesting inventions occurred during these period. We are fortunate as a nation that friends and family were able to give him supportive therapy without any specialized college training and free of charge. Otherwise our Constitution would not be the same. Madison and some of the other founding fathers might have been able to write that document, but it's Jefferson's masterpiece.

It used to be common knowledge that idleness is not good for recovering from depression. In the past, it was known most people had periods of depression, based on the trials of life.

Now there is so much boredom connected with mental health treatment, that it seems this knowledge has been forgotten. When it was known that everyone had some of these periods of sadness there was therefore not as much stigma attached to it as there is now.

We've been conditioned to believe that if people would only stay on their medications, their troubles would go away. In the 19th century, when drummers plied the Old West with their "miracle" nostrums, they were strung up if their claims didn't come true. It was swift justice. Not so in the Prozac revolution.

It took more than a decade to get the black box warning labels passed. But that also had to be a compromise with the FDA. It's stunning that an agency charged with ultimate public health would allow the drug companies to influence any of their decisions. But when the kind of profit made by these meds is involved, public health can easily be compromised.

The fact that children are the only ones included in the warning of increased suicide is fascinating. Can the FDA really claim that the teenager's brain is that much different than any adults?

So few psychiatrists joined this truth movement in terms of percentage that one has to wonder about the advice they give about any aspect of the life of their patients.

It doesn't take a brilliant epidemiologist to know the damage these meds were doing to the metabolism, gastric and muscular systems of the body. I could watch the muscles in my legs contract and expand in rhythmic fashion when at rest. That always bothered me, although it was not painful.

To continue to claim deep empathy for patients while referring them to a rash of specialists for iatrogenic illnesses seems a crime to me. The fact that so many patients using an SSRI need to see other doctors, is a factor in the growing cost of medicine. Yet the patient was never told that the source of their declining health was these medications. Stress related diseases became a watchword for the nation.

It seems like psychiatrists became masters of deceit in order to keep the Prozac revolution going. The continuing strength of these medications on the stock market made it easy to justify all of the common and sometimes very painful side effects.

But covering up the link between suicide and a substance the public was duped into believing would solve all their problems, ought to bring out the vigilante spirit that was much more effective than the incestuous and corrupt gang at the FDA.

That no reporter saw the callousness of the continuing excuse of "underlying mental illness" ought to have caused many more alarms to ring than it did.

I tried to ask my doctor that question every time I'd see a report of some grizzly suicide on television. My most common question was "underlying illness? What are antidepressants supposed to prevent?"

"Scans of the brain show that these drugs stimulate the brain in the area thought responsible for depression." A serious look always accompanied this statement, as though he was lecturing a group of freshmen.

"If I was taking an antibiotic for tonsillitis and still couldn't swallow, I would hope that you might assume that the medication wasn't helping."

"It's not the same thing."

I'm sorry to say this, but communicating with people who get paid for their listening skills is just like this. Yet, due to the unending propaganda on our public media, we still listen to their advice on "communicating."

.

.

Chapter Fourteen – Joy Comes in the Morning

In *Against Therapy*, Masson recommends trusting friends rather than therapists for depression. In a society so saturated with advice about getting professional help as soon as possible, this is hard to do.

But I thank God I found the right friend in the months after Jerry's suicide. It was a gruesome death and his body wasn't even discovered for several weeks. It was so badly decomposed, the entry wound could not be determined and the date of death given by the Medical Examiner was within a twenty four hour framework.

But because of Evelyn, I didn't get severely depressed. Grief is never easy, and I had my times of trial. Had I not known the story behind the long fight to tell the truth about the dangers of antidepressants, I might have returned to treatment.

I might have convinced myself that despite all the ethics complaints I'd had to file, I might actually find an honest therapist. But I decided not to take the chance that my extreme pain over Jerry's death might be taken advantage of. What had been my lesson following rape?

The pain from his suicide was so deep and wide that I desperately wanted relief. But every time I even thought about getting help, I simply climbed the five flights of stairs to my apartment. Never could I do such a thing while on those meds.

I also wondered how many more diagnoses I might be given if I didn't do grief in precisely the way a therapist might decide to be normal. So many of those diagnoses had no basis in fact. Just the fact that I'd stayed sober through rape, all the betrayal by unethical therapists, cancer, and now Jerry's suicide, argues against eight of my twelve diagnoses. My long sobriety is never mentioned in my records. Anything that challenges those punitive diagnoses never appears in my records. Blood tests in those records show no alcohol or street drugs in my blood stream year after year.

In Touched by Fire, by Kay Jamison Bailey, a detailed description of Bi-Polar Disorder is given. That's one of those punitive diagnoses I was given. I did not receive that diagnosis until after my 54th birthday. Bailey says almost 95% of patients with this mental illness start having symptoms very early in life. Most are diagnosed before their mid-twenties.

She states that very few patients with that diagnosis can remain sober for very long. They also tend to have a frenzied sleep. I very seldom have a sleepless night. When that does happen, it's usually because of some trauma like not getting a refill for diabetes medication with only five tablets remaining.

During manic periods, family and friends either bring them to the emergency room for treatment, or police are called. This is a long-standing pattern for most Bi-Polars. Bailey should know about this disorder, since this is her diagnosis.

I have never had even one driving under the influence arrest. I began attending Adult Children of Alcoholics twenty two years ago, and then voluntarily quit drinking through Alcoholics Anonymous. My father died at the age of forty, from a coronary.

He had acquired rheumatic fever as a child and then tuberculosis shortly after high school. But his alcoholism was one of the factors in his death. That was also true of Jerry. His drinking problem was an underlying cause of his suicide, I think. For though he had gotten almost four years of sobriety, and had been able to get his license back and buy a used car, the disease of alcoholism never loses control entirely. No one was informed of his plans to commit suicide, so no one can be sure of his reasons.

But he helped me deal with the issues around my surgery for precancerous cells in the vagina. I chose him because of certain family issues with other family members. He was not involved in those issues. It was so shortly after my surgery that his body was found, that my major reaction was "why didn't he call?"

My personal reaction to this deep pain was to reflect on my childhood. In therapy, I had gone over all those painful memories so many times that I decided to focus on the positive memories of that period of my life. Therapy takes so much out of context, this decision was almost revolutionary.

The most positive person in those early years was my Great Aunt Alma. She was a refugee worker in Rangoon, Burma, and spy for the U.S. State Department during the Second World War. Her biography had never been written. I could not get to the small town in which most of her papers were stored, so I decided to write a novel about some of the facts of her life.

After the first draft was written, I decided to try adapting it into a movie script. I'd never taken a course in that type of writing and couldn't afford to do so now. I simply joined a screenwriter's group. I'd already finished a first draft, getting formatting advice from library books.

The vice president of this group of semi-professional screenwriters did an evaluation of my script and was very complimentary about Taming the Dragon. His suggestions for improvements were very brief and were completed within a few months after joining the group. It is this script that won a consolation prize within a few months of Jerry's death.

If I were even half as crazy as my medical records portray me to be, how could I get the Vice President of a Screenwriter's Group to do an evaluation for free? I'm supposed to have tremendous problems with authority figures, and artists are known for stormy relationships. Yet he was very kind in his criticisms of Taming the Dragon. And I was very appreciative.

Though I had just returned to the faith of my childhood, I also started writing gospel lyrics. When I prayed for help with the grief, these marvelous lyrics just began occurring. Whole songs, with words and music, just popped into my mind. They made staying focused on the positives in life, very easy.

Two of Evelyn's children had been part-time musicians, so she easily gave me encouragement about the music. I'd never studied music and needed to find someone with whom to collaborate in order to have anything worth submitting anywhere. Neither of Evelyn's sons had ever done any sacred music, so they weren't able to assist me.

I found that staying focused on the positives in my life, was better than discussing all the deep pain I was feeling from Jerry's suicide. I also learned that talking about it made it more real.

Evelyn had lost a child to drowning when he was in grade school, so she knew that one never really gets closure. It just becomes less and less painful over time.

You never stop wondering if there was more that you might have done. It just isn't a daily question after a while. Since we now have "grief experts," no one is allowed to do this very personal thing that we all have in common, in their own way.

The stages of grief are now categorized like items in a grocery store. If you don't pass through them in the exact pattern described by "grief experts," you don't do grief correctly.

When I really needed to discuss the issues around his death, Evelyn could find some time. It didn't define our friendship, however. *It's time to close*, was not in her vocabulary, but I didn't call her after midnight, either.

This seemed to totally challenge everything therapy was supposed to be about. Analyzing every mood and behavior was supposed to bring insight necessary for change. I now knew how wrong that notion was. Writing this and accessing all the pain I'd live through all over again, has made that all the more clear.

And since no aspect of human life has escaped analysis by psychotherapists, I knew I didn't want another half dozen punitive diagnoses based on the way I do grief. It can't be that people do things differently, based on culture, learning, spirituality, or who they are. And though psychiatrists and psychologists have a diagnostic manual that is almost four inches thick, defining the essence of human beings is still a nebulous thing.

People used to be allowed to go through grief in their own way. Now one is told to go to a doctor and get on some drug. Suicide survivors groups have proliferated. Do they really help anyone, or is it just another way for a therapist to pay their bills?

Does someone not connected to your loss in any way have any real interest in how it's affected you? At the end of the day, the "grief expert" goes home and doesn't even think about the group that day. It's just a job to them.

A friendship is much different. Friends can admit that they are just as puzzled by life's challenges as you are. With a friend, you don't have to worry about whether the insurance will cover the bill. Their opinions are just that. They therefore represent real affection.

Evelyn helped keep me doing positive things, just by being genuinely enthusiastic. We laughed about stupid things her pets were doing everyday, and I found out I could trust her with anything.

Not only did she help with the grief over Jerry's suicide, but also the anger over unethical therapists I'd known. She had been a ward secretary for one of the major hospitals in the Twin Cities, and had many an amusing story about egotistical doctors. Most of the lyrics I wrote were in praise to Jesus. Every day I found a reason to sing. My faith got stronger though I'd been through a cancer scare and a suicide in less than three months. I should have been unable to function if even half of the diagnoses on my records had any basis in reality.

I've said this before, in several ways, but it was during this time that it became clearest to me. I ought to have been bedridden with depression, and frantic over my health and future. My cancer had made me face my own mortality, and my brother's death had added to that burden in ways I can't express.

But instead of becoming more fragile, I found a new way to blossom. Though there were four music instructors in the church I was attending, I could not get anyone to write the music for my lyrics. One person promised but then could not find time in her schedule in more than eight months.

I began singing in public at this time, hoping to find someone who might know someone. The purpose of this live country group was not to make those kinds of connections. It was supposed to allow people from the audience, who'd never tried singing in front of anyone before, to try their wings.

I'd had an ulterior motive other than acquiring a possible accompanist: public evidence with which to challenge some of those punitive diagnoses. I found the applause from the audience for my Patsy Cline medley so rejuvenating as I grieved Jerry's death that it became like a special blessing. I loved it.

I was accepted by the band and audience. No one could tell that I was any different than anyone else in the auditorium. If they could have seen my medical records, they would never have wanted me to sit next to them. And I wouldn't have blamed any of them.

It became so much fun that I would only miss it if I had a high fever, injury or flu. Whether sitting and just listening to the live music, or performing my brief medley, it inspired me. It also inspired even more lyrics.

So to find an accompanist, I turned to another friend who had recently married a retired country performer. His career had never gained him national attention, but he was very talented anyway.

I'd never met Don Merckling before the summer of 2003. But he found the time to write the music for my first compact disc, Dakota Faith. He not only played guitar and dobro, but also banjo and steel guitar, so he was able to record all parts of a band behind my lyrics.

At about that time, I had my second surgery for cancer and decided that I wanted to leave Minnesota. I had been thinking about moving closer to Washington D.C. to be closer to my son, who lives in Frederick, MD, which is near Gettysburg, PA. The online Washington Post had about five times as many writing positions as any Twin Cities' paper.

An unexpected rent increase was part of the impetus. Though I'd seen an arbitrator and was told that the amount was not right, I wanted to leave. I could have stayed where I was, but one of my hopes was that if I were closer to my son, some of the hard times of the soul would be easier.

Just being able to have him over for supper occasionally, was something to look forward to, also. My heart was broken after Jerry's death, and I thought a change of scenery might also help with those issues and memories.

So shortly after Dakota Faith was recorded, I left Minnesota and stayed with a cousin, who lived near a naval base near Washington D.C. Some things can't be organized through the Internet, and the only transitional housing I could find was for veterans and located in the Washington D.C. ghetto. So after six weeks, I reluctantly returned to Minnesota.

But I was able to move cross-country twice in less than a year, cope with the disappointment that resulted from not finding work or housing close to my son, yet stay focused on my future. My cousin was very kind to me, and is still a good friend. Spending six weeks closer to my son was also a wonderful gift. But it didn't end as I'd hoped.

By this time Don's health had deteriorated and he could no longer perform any music. I began attending a songwriter's group that met once a month. One of the other members promised to write the music for my remaining lyrics. I would sing my lyrics a Capella, before this group and be blessed with spontaneous applause.

Again another year had passed and no music had been written. The applause for my lyrics had been a priceless gift, but my lack of money became a problem.

So I turned to another friend – one I've known for more than forty years. My medical records now state that I can't sustain relationships for more than a few months. I'm supposed to be only capable of very intense and fragile relationships. But the son of this friend will write the music and perform these songs. He's a choir director at his church, so my lyrics will get the best possible attention and will be recorded at no cost to me.

If I were even half as manipulative of people as my records say, I could not have found even one person with whom to collaborate. I also could not have found a friend like Evelyn to listen to my pain after Jerry's suicide.

Have I healed from the grief or the nonsense of unethical and dishonest therapists? I doubt it. But at least I have friends who believe in me.

Epilogue

In preparing to write this book, I re-contacted the numerous agencies supposedly charged with oversight of the mental health system. I did this in part to ensure that I would be fairer to all of these agencies than they had been to me. Also, more than two years had passed since my last attempt at justice. I wanted to make sure that no changes had occurred while I had been working on my own life, in my own way.

I've said this before, but it bears repeating anyway. In those two years, I'd become a cancer and a suicide survivor. I'd moved cross-country twice, without raising any eyebrows. All of these incredible stressors should have resulted in some severe public difficulties. Someone close to me ought to have called the police and had me court ordered to treatment.

Even in the one circumstance, when a sudden drop in blood pressure resulted in an escort by police to the hospital, I still could not be court ordered. I was unconscious on admission to that hospital, and more than two and a half years have transpired since then. I was discharged against medical advice. I have nevertheless remained drug free. The only medication I take on a daily basis is Metformin.

That brings us to an interesting development pertaining to MPLS VA hospital. It has to do with the fact that I was referred to the Patient Behavior Committee, after my angry reaction to a patient representative when MPLS VA refused to refill Metformin.

I was told to wait for an appointment that was more than thirty days in the future, and I had only five days of medication remaining. To ensure that I would live, I used my Medicare benefits to obtain a refill from the county hospital. (Young veterans returning from combat might not have this option.)

I was summoned by letter with an official looking stationery and logo for the Patient Behavior Committee. When I called the doctor listed as president of this committee, I was told that the PBC had been "in existence for seventeen years and hundreds of veterans had been disciplined by this committee."

Yet, Lori Suvalsky, MD was not able to provide by-laws, agendas, rules for the committee, or any other corroboration for the history of this committee. I then filed a Freedom of Information Act request for common office documents a real committee would file through the federal procurement system. I asked for the first file cabinet ever purchased, the first typewriter or computer, the first box of paper clips, and one requisition for common office supplies for every year since it was formed.

Supposedly, the PBC does not need a file cabinet, computer, standardized forms, or any other office supplies. I have never heard of such a thing in the federal system. Most committees and agencies in the U.S. system are commonly known for their penchant to purchase items at the end of each fiscal year, to ensure their continuation as a bona-fide committee or agency.

An agency that disciplines veterans with regularity can't honor their confidentiality without at least having a safe place to store the results of their decisions, can it?

On my other major issue pertaining to a doctor in MPLS VA, I re-contacted the Medical Practice Board. I wanted to hear their reasons for denying my claim against Eric Dieperinck, MD and his diagnosis of Personality 8. The executive director, Robert Leach, freely expressed his anger when questioned about the board's refusal to investigate that claim. He said, "I don't care."

"That's exactly right," I said. "The board doesn't care about patient rights at all." Though its website states that it will investigate all legitimate claims, it seems much more likely that it will protect the medical community against all perceived attacks.

Mr. Leach is certainly not alone in not caring. That seems true across the board. One after another, the licensing boards and state agencies charged with oversight, seldom act on behalf of the client when gross injustice occurs.

Another case in point is Kathy Dohmeier, in the state agency, Ombudsman for Mental Health. Taxpayers are funding its mission, which is supposed to be assisting mental health clients in obtaining something nearing justice from this system, when there is a dispute of any legitimate sort.

But Ms. Dohmeier doesn't even know that Legal Aide will not take any case that might result in a monetary award for any client. She referred me to Legal Aide to file malpractice pertaining to Personality 8, without even knowing that agency's rules.

Nor did she seem to know that complainants who file malpractice suits must pay expert witness fees out of pocket. The client will be paid back when the award is finally paid. But one needs an executive position and a house to mortgage to pay these expert witness fees. Someone on social security simply does not have the financial means to file malpractice.

Doctors in this state know this, and act accordingly. Also, malpractice attorneys I contacted in the twin cities before filing my initial complaint with the Medical Practice Board, laughed at representing me.

Part of the reason for that is, the lawyers representing the insurance company will overwhelm their paralegals with documents during the discovery phase of the pending trial. The recent caps on awards make medical malpractice almost impossible for this reason. Apparently Ms. Dohmeier didn't know this either, though her job description requires some knowledge of the choices she recommends for clients of her agency.

This is why psychiatrists, psychologists and social workers behave as they please in the mental health system. Most of them sneer at the rules that are supposed to ensure some rights for their clients or patients. Either that, or they turn the other way when abuses occur.

And yes, I do deeply regret ever having agreed to seek professional help following rape. I never would have had this awful, heartless education had I refused treatment, like every sex offender is allowed to do in this state.

Are the laws similar in every state? I can't say, but Minnesota advertises itself as the very best place in the U.S. to get professional help for any of life's many traumas.

Bibliography

Toxic Psychiatry. Peter Breggin, MD. St. Martin's Press: NY 1992.
Against Therapy. Jeffrey Masson, MD. Atheneum: NY. 1995.
Listening to Prozac. Peter Kramer, MD. Random House: NY 1988.
Prozac Backlash. Joseph McMullen. Viking Press: NY 1998.
Antidepressant Survival Program. Robert S. Haedaya, MD. Random House: NY, 2000.

End Notes

Chapter One:

[1] Rape and Sexual Assault Center, 2431 Hennepin Ave, MPLS
[2] Rodriguez: History of a Sexual Assault Predator. By Mara H. Gottfried, St. Paul Pioneer Press.
[3] Minnesota Civil Commitment Act pp 34-36

Chapter Three:

[1] Against Therapy, Jeffrey Masson, MD Atheneum 1990 p. 22-24
[2] Ibid, 1990, p. 33-35
[3] Toxic Psychiatry, Peter Breggin, MD St Martin's Press 1990
[4] Against Therapy, Jeffrey Masson, Atheneum, 1990 p.56-57
[5] Ibid p. 131
[6] Let Them Eat Prozac, David Healey, MD Simonton, Toronto, 2003, p. 24
[7] Ibid, pg 45

Chapter Seven:

[1] The Age of Anxiety, Thomas Szasz, Viking Press NY p 45

Chapter Eight:

[1] Listening to Prozac, Peter Kramer, MD Random House, NY 1993 p 35

[2] Against Therapy, Jeffrey Masson, Atheneum, NY 1995 p 185

[3] Challenge of the Borderline, Jeffrey Kroll, Random House, NY p44

[4] Let Them Eat Prozac, David Healey, Simonton, Toronto, 2003 p37

[5] Against Therapy, Jeffrey Masson, MD Atheneum, NY. 1995 p 142

[6] Prozac Backlash, Joseph McMullen, MD. Viking Press, NY 1998 p.25

[7] Prozac Backlash, Joseph McMullen, MD. Viking Press NY 1998 p 43

[8] Getting Your Life Back, Jesse Wright, Simon & Shuster NY 1993 p 54

[9] Let Them Eat Prozac, David Healey, Simonton, Toronto, 2003

[10] The Antidepressant Survival Program, David Haedaya, Scriveners, NY 2000 p 11

[11] Against Therapy, Jeffrey Masson, Atheneum NY 1995 p 203

Chapter Ten:

[1] Hypoglycemia: Pathophysiology, Diagnosis and Treatment, Phillip Cryer, MD Oxford University Press, 1997 p 6

Chapter Thirteen:

[1] Against Therapy, Jeffrey Masson, Atheneum, NY 1990 p 57

[2] Toxic Psychiatry, Peter Breggin, MD St. Martin's Press, 1990, p54

www.ingramcontent.com/pod-product-compliance
Lightning Source LLC
Chambersburg PA
CBHW031950190326
41519CB00007B/742